LeBRON
JAMES

LeBron James

The Rise of a Star

David Lee Morgan, Jr.

GRAY & COMPANY, PUBLISHERS · CLEVELAND

Gray & Company, Publishers
1588 E. 40th St., Cleveland, OH 44103
(216) 431-2665
www.grayco.com

Morgan, David Lee, Jr.
Lebron James / by David Lee Morgan, Jr.
p. cm.
1.James, Lebron. 2. Basketball players—United States—
Biography. I. Title.
GV884.J36M67 2003796.323'092—dc21
2003011495

ISBN 1-886228-74-4
First Edition
Printed in the United States of America

CONTENTS

"Basketball is basically my life, and if I told you something different, I'd be telling you a lie."

—LeBron James

ONE

BIG NIGHT

On December 12, 2002, a near-sellout crowd of more than 11,000 fans streamed from the cold, dark Cleveland evening into the bright light and swelling noise of the downtown CSU Convocation Center. It was a big night. They were there to watch a high school kid from a small parochial school in nearby Akron play basketball.

They would not be the only ones watching. A television crew from ESPN2 was there with the network's top announcers to broadcast the game nationwide. Reporters from local and national newspapers, including the *New York Times* and *USA Today*, were on hand to cover the story—both the on-court action and the hive of activity buzzing around it.

Why the big fuss over 17-year-old LeBron James?

He was "The Chosen One." That was how *Sports Illustrated* had labeled this tall, charismatic teen when the magazine of record in the sports world made him only the eighth high school ballplayer to appear on its cover in 48 years. LeBron had been touted widely—and wildly—by many sports insiders as one of the best high school basketball player ever. Maybe *the* best. Ever.

This night was his chance to prove it. Would he truly shine as a legitimate star, ready to make the huge jump directly to the NBA? Or would he disappoint, revealing, as critics complained, that this kid had been extravagantly overrated?

LeBron was already on a first-name basis with Northeast Ohio; he had been making headlines locally since his sophomore year. And he was well known to the small community of serious high school basketball fans throughout the U.S., who knew him as a natural talent and a tough competitor. But this night, before a packed house and a large national television audience, would be his coming-out party.

"Dickie V! Dickie V!"

For a moment the cries of the basketball fans in the arena were as deafening as the man standing courtside, smiling happily at his fans.

"Dickie V! Dickie V!"

Dick Vitale, the iconic face and unstoppable voice of big-time college basketball, had walked onto the floor with his ESPN2 colleagues.

If you were a stranger to the game, you might have thought Vitale was the reason these fans were jammed onto the bleachers overlooking the basketball court. After all, the teams were only high school students. The announcer was a star, and obviously a fan favorite. Dickie V loved the games, loved the kids, and wanted everyone to be a winner.

Beside him were NBA hall-of-famer Bill Walton, still tall and powerful looking, the opposite of Vitale with a matter-of-fact delivery and expressions ranging from deadpan to deader-pan.

With them was Dan Shulman, who loved sports and had found his dream job as a reporter. He would fill in moments of silence if Vitale and Walton ever paused to catch their breaths.

"I hope Dan isn't getting paid by the word, because he won't make any money," Vitale joked.

The hype and hoopla generated by the event did not excite everyone.

Veteran CBS Sports basketball analyst Billy Packer had gone on the record in opposition to this particular event and to the televised promotion of high school kids in general.

"Well, television is a business but I am very much against the promotion of high school athletes as if they have accomplished something beyond high school athleticism, and if I were assigned to do that game I wouldn't broadcast it," Packer said.

Packer had been involved with basketball for many years and had seen many prodigies who never quite succeeded in the majors. He thought high school players needed a few years of college to mature.

Of LeBron James he said, "Let him win a state high school basketball championship before we name him the greatest high school player to come out of Ohio."

He had a good point. However in this particular case, he might have been wrong. To begin with, LeBron and his teammates had already won *two* state championships. But it wasn't just the two championships that made LeBron different. This youngster displayed such genuine poise, charm, and maturity that most who had watched him closely over the past three years agreed he had the polish of a professional already.

As LeBron prepared for the night's game alongside his teammates, he wasn't thinking about other people's expectations for him. His own were great enough. This game was special to him for reasons more important than television crews. He had vowed to himself, months before, to win this game for his teammates and himself, and to redeem himself for two of his most disappointing defeats.

LeBron's school, St. Vincent-St. Mary High School of Akron, Ohio, was a small urban Catholic school usually known more for its academics than for its sports teams. The school had lucked into basketball glory when LeBron and his four closest friends enrolled together, bringing the core of a team like none the school had ever seen before.

That night, the St. Vincent-St. Mary Fighting Irish were facing mighty Oak Hill Academy, a prep school from Mouth of Wilson, Virginia that was a perennial national powerhouse with rosters filled with top Division I college basketball prospects. The two teams had faced one another twice in the two previous seasons, and the Irish had lost both times.

During LeBron's sophomore year, St. Vincent-St. Mary played Oak Hill in the National Hoops Classic at Battelle Hall in downtown Columbus, Ohio. The Oak Hill Warriors should have dominated the court, with six players on their roster who would go on to play Division I college ball. The Irish surprised them, though, and took a lead into the third quarter—only to lose at the buzzer on a missed shot by LeBron, who was devastated to have let his team down.

The Irish lost the rematch the following year, at the Prime Time Shootout in Trenton, New Jersey. Oak Hill's team then featured guard Carmelo Anthony, who would go on to help Syracuse University win an NCAA championship. LeBron and Carmelo became friendly rivals. LeBron had the better game, scoring a game-high 36 points to Carmelo's 34, but Carmelo got the last laugh as Oak Hill defeated St. Vincent-St. Mary 72-68.

Now in his senior year, this would be LeBron's final shot at proving his team could take on, and beat, the very best.

"I can't wait for the game. I'm going to put on a show," LeBron predicted.

The event had an electric air of anticipation, with all the energy of a big-time NBA contest.

The star of the show took center stage, wearing his emerald-green Nike shoes and his emerald headband with the prominent NBA logo right on the front. The crowd was primed to witness athletic greatness in the raw.

During the pregame warmup, LeBron put on a show. He indulged in high-flying acrobatics, moving as though boosted by springs in his shoes.

But then, when the game finally started, LeBron seemed to have forgotten everything he had learned about playing under pressure. He tried too hard, used too much muscle, and missed his first few shots. You could almost see Oak Hill's players relax slightly, as though the one player they feared the most might actually be weakening under the tension of the moment.

Eventually, LeBron remembered to relax. He settled down and began making shot after shot, including a spectacular dunk that would be shown repeatedly on ESPN's nightly highlights show, *SportsCenter*, the following day. LeBron scored 31 points, grabbed 13 rebounds, and dished out 6 assists. When the buzzer finally sounded and the team looked at the scoreboard, they had done more than win. They had bested the best, No. 1-ranked Oak Hill, by 20 points, 65-45.

Dick Vitale stared at the score, stared at LeBron, then declared to the camera, "He's the truth, the whole truth and nothing but the truth."

What Vitale and many of the others who were watching LeBron for the first time didn't know, though, was that the

truth, the whole truth about LeBron James, was not his spectacular performance on the court that night. He had indeed
arrived, but natural talent and competitive drive alone had not
propelled him here, had not alone led this inner-city youth
from poverty, steered him from the all-too familiar temptations of the streets, and inspired him to discover his desire and
ability to lead others to victory.

The story behind the young phenom's remarkable success
was visible all around him in the arena that night—alongside
him on the court, on the sidelines, and in the stands. The truth
is, without his teammates, his mentors, his friends, his family,
LeBron James would never have been there at all.

Sharing the spotlight with him in the afterglow of their win
were LeBron's teammates and best friends—Dru Joyce III,
Willie McGee, Romeo Travis, and Sian Cotton—the "Fab Five,"
they were now being called, who had grown up together as
they played together (some of them for as many as eight
years), and who had learned to rely on one another on and off
the court. No one ballplayer can win a game, let alone a season, without a team, but these particular boys were more than
supporting players. "They are my brothers," LeBron insisted,
truly meaning it.

At courtside was LeBron's coach, Dru Joyce III, who was
leading the St. Vincent-St. Mary Irish toward their third state
championship in four years. He was not only a coach, he was
extended family; he had been closely involved with LeBron
and his own son, "Little Dru," since the fifth grade.

In the stands were hundreds representing St. Vincent-St.
Mary, the parochial school where teachers made sure students
knew that sports came third, academics came second, and life
came first. LeBron was pleasing many of them far more with
his good grades and his good behavior than with his slam

dunks. LeBron's fellow students teased him at school like any-one else, and they valued him as much for "Best Smile" as "Most Athletic."

Frankie Walker, Sr. was watching nearby, too. He had been the first to place a real basketball into LeBron's hands and try to teach him the right way to play the game. But more impor-tantly, he and his family at the same time opened their home to LeBron just when the young boy was most at risk of losing his way.

Not able to attend, but present in spirit and watching the game on television was Keith Dambrot. The former Division I college coach had once been laid low by scandal, only to dis-cover budding basketball genius in the young LeBron while coaching as volunteer at Akron's downtown Jewish Commu-nity Center. Then, by chance, he got to coach LeBron and the rest of the Fab Five to St. Vincent-St. Mary's first two state championships. Dambrot had helped LeBron build a career—and LeBron helped him resurrect his own.

Finally, sitting together in the stands were LeBron's mother, Gloria, and her good friend, the man LeBron called dad, Eddie Jackson.

Eddie was a charming hustler, a man who had served time in prison for selling drugs (and would soon do time again for fraud). But he loved Gloria, adored her son, and vowed to al-ways be there for LeBron. He didn't always succeed, but LeBron loved him for his effort.

Gloria had become a single parent in high school and never really found her footing. She and little LeBron drifted, living with friends and neighbors, trying to get by. But her love, at least, was steady and ample, and Gloria managed to gather an extraordinary extended family to help nurture the boy. She was fiercely protective of her "baby" and always found a way to get him what he needed. As he grew older, LeBron would joke that because of their ages, they were almost like sister and brother. Regardless, the two were devoted to each other.

After the game that December night, buffeted by media all wanting to interview him about his team's high-profile win, LeBron James looked calm and cool, every bit the smooth professional. He had good reason to be comfortable: he was at home on the basketball court, and surrounded by all his family.

HICKORY STREET

Gloria James never talked about the youth who got her pregnant. When you're sixteen years old and suddenly realize you've been racing too fast through life, priorities change. One day she was dreaming of getting her driver's license, of parties, proms, and graduation. The next she was trying to care for a helpless infant, trying to get enough sleep until her newborn son might at last get through the night without a feeding, a diaper change, or just needing to be comforted.

Life had been hard before; now it got harder.

Freda James, Gloria's mother, was a realist. In previous generations, parents might have forced a teen marriage—to "give the baby a name." But Freda knew there was a difference between making a baby and being able to parent. And as far as Freda was concerned, her daughter's child already had a name—LeBron *James*. She would help her daughter nurture and love that child with the fierceness of someone who had already struggled through poverty and disrespect her entire life, clinging with pride to the accomplishments others might overlook because they didn't know how hard she had worked to achieve them.

Gloria was one of three children and the only daughter. Her brothers, Terry and Curt, had always looked out for their only sister. Now that she was going to be a teenage mom, they realized how important it was for them to take care of her, more like fathers, because their own father was out of the picture.

They all lived together on Akron's Hickory Street, in an elderly house on which Freda continually struggled to pay the mortgage. Now, Gloria brought her new son home to join the family.

Hickory Street was one of those neighborhoods where tough times settled in long before the rest of the city realized there were problems and lingered long after they had worn out their welcome and been evicted everywhere else. Most of the residents earned minimum wage, maybe a little better, and because they were frequently under-educated for the jobs available in the area they were often among the first to be unemployed when the economy was bad. They learned to work together, to help one another. Neighbors would occasionally take in the young children of couples who were having hard times, and everyone watched out for each other as best they could.

Hickory Street wasn't the most desirable place to live in the city—in fact, it was little better than the worst public housing project—but the people who lived on that street were proud of their neighborhood. Freda James especially. Many of their houses, though old, were nicely painted, some with colorful flowers planted near the front porch. Having little income didn't always mean the people on Hickory didn't care about who they were or where they came from.

"That was our home," Gloria said.

Yet even its location seemed to work against Hickory Street. Hickory Street was in a valley. Up the hill just a few blocks was the far more affluent Merriman Road, where there were beautiful, sprawling homes with manicured lawns that seemed to stretch as far back as football fields. The paved driveways often ended with a flat area in front of an NBA regulation basketball hoop on the garage.

Down on Hickory Street, the basketball hoop was a milk crate, hung precariously on a telephone pole by a few nails— at whatever height the tallest available boy could reach.

People would throw their trash down the hill toward Hickory Street. As you drove along the street, you'd see, in the vacant or wooded lots, old tires and refrigerators and bathtubs and other refuse dumped at night illegally by inconsiderate people who didn't want to pay to have their oversized trash hauled away.

To many in Akron, Hickory Street was all about discards, including the people who lived there.

Freda James didn't worry about how the rest of the world viewed her and her family. She had compassion for the lonely and the hurting herself. She opened her home to anyone who was trying to move beyond the often self-created troubles of the young.

Eddie Jackson was typical of the youngsters Freda took in. He was one of those boys who seemed to peak in high school, then never be quite able to move beyond. A natural athlete, he excelled in all sports but was best known in for his success in track and field at Akron's Buchtel High School.

Eddie came into Gloria and Freda's life when LeBron was eight months old, racing through diapers and trying to pull himself upright. At 20, Eddie was close in age to Terry, and torn between trying to become a responsible adult and working the street for faster money than you could get punching a time clock.

There was something sweet about Eddie, a sensitivity most boys won't normally reveal.

Eddie and Gloria started dating when Gloria was in high school and LeBron was eight months old. To the adults around him, Eddie was obviously lost in life, uncertain where to go or what to do with himself, and his plight touched Freda's heart. Freda was seriously ill (though her family didn't know it), but so long as she had strength, she was going to help her children, her grandchild, and anyone else who needed her. She let Eddie move into her home with her sons and daughter while he and Gloria were dating. He needed a place to stay, and Freda wanted to fill his need.

"To meet Gloria's mother, you would've met the most wonderful person in the world," Eddie said. "What parent would let their daughter's boyfriend stay with them in the same house? That's the type of lady Freda was. If she trusted you, she loved you. If she didn't, she'd tell you to get the hell out of her face. And Gloria is the same way."

Eddie quickly grew attached to LeBron, though there were days when he wasn't sure he would survive the little boy's play. LeBron was a fan of WWF wrestling, the violent soap opera of televised sports. He would imitate his favorite, Randy "Macho Man" Savage. "You could be laying on the floor and the next thing you know LeBron is jumping up and down on the couch and he'd jump right on you," Eddie said.

LeBron mastered the wrestling lingo, too, shouting things like, "I'm coming off the top rope" before flying through the air for a body slam on Eddie. But he couldn't say his words clearly yet, and they sounded more like comedian Eddie Murphy's impression of Buckwheat from the *Our Gang* comedies—"I'm tummin' op da top wope. I'm tummin' op da top wope."

Eddie would tell LeBron to go sit down somewhere, and the toddler would—for about a minute. Then he'd grab a football and run into the wall at top speed, stunning himself. "He looked like one of those Looney Toons cartoon characters who got hit by something and were seeing stars circle around their head," Eddie said.

LeBron was nearly three years old when he got his first basketball. But the event that in retrospect might seem to forecast such a bright future was then steeped in sorrow for the family.

Gloria was working at Children's Palace, a large toy store, and Eddie had a job as a manager at Waterbed City. For Christmas, they decided to get LeBron a toy basketball set—ball, hoop, backboard, and stand—because LeBron was almost as fascinated by basketball as he was by wrestling.

On Christmas Eve, with LeBron in bed, the hoop was set up and the other gifts were scattered all about. Then Eddie and Gloria went to Gloria's cousin's house for a Christmas Eve party.

It was about three o'clock in the morning on Christmas Day, Gloria and Eddie back home and getting ready for bed, when Eddie heard a thump. He ran into the kitchen where he found Freda on the floor. She had never told her family that she was sick. She just kept going, day to day, until the moment when she had a massive heart attack.

Eddie gently raised Freda from the floor, cradling her in his arms as Gloria called for help. It was too late. Freda passed her last breath as the young man who had become so much a part of the family held her in his arms.

"It was tough," Eddie said. Freda was just 42 years old, a young woman who should have had years more of life. Instead, the heart so filled with love for others had failed her body. "Anytime you lose your mother, it's tough. That's why those pictures we took of LeBron on Christmas Day were so special, because LeBron is jumping around and enjoying Christmas and he had no idea that his grandmother had died earlier that morning. We wanted to make things as normal for him as possible."

So, unknowing, on Christmas morning LeBron opened up his gift, saw the basketball hoop, and went crazy. He started playing with it immediately, though he didn't quite understand the concept of shooting the ball through the basket. He would just run with the ball to the hoop, dunk it, and knock over the whole set.

"Me and Gloria are looking at him run that thing over, so we raised it up so he would start shooting at it, instead of knocking the thing over," Eddie said. "But all he would do is start back from the living room, run through the dining room and he was still dunking the ball. I was thinking, *man this kid has some elevation for just being three years old.*"

"LeBron would be in his diaper, dunking all over that rim," Terry James recalled, laughing.

That was the joy of their painful Christmas, and Eddie took pictures all day. He wanted to make sure he captured LeBron's happiness.

Freda's death left the three James' children, Gloria, Terry and Curtis, in an emotional crisis.

"I ain't going to lie to you, after our mother died, it was hectic," Terry said. "The money wasn't right and our house got old and ragged and they tore the house down. But I made sure Gloria and LeBron always had a place to stay."

Terry was 22, Gloria was 19, and Curt was 12.

Curt admitted that he had a tough time dealing with his mother's death. "All of us had it rough when my mother died. I couldn't take it. I didn't have any guidance and it made me slip.

I didn't have anybody on my back making sure I did the right things."

But, he said, "All I knew was that I wasn't going to let my nephew mess up. We were all going to make sure he didn't have to go through what we went through."

Neighbors on Hickory Street knew that, with Freda gone, there were children raising children in the James home. Many of them pitched in to make sure little LeBron had what he needed in the way of food and clothing.

One of those neighbors was Wanda Reaves. Her home, much like Freda James's had been, was one where everyone in the neighborhood felt safe and comfortable when they visited. And it smelled like she always had something good cooking on the stove.

"LeBron and Gloria have always been fans of my cooking," Reaves said proudly. "LeBron is a big boy, and he can really eat." She had known Gloria since she was a baby, and her heart went out to Freda's daughter and grandson. "No one there could keep up the house so it was condemned. LeBron was four or five, and all I can tell you is that despite all of that, Gloria was very devoted to LeBron. They were devoted to each other."

Despite the help of neighbors, though, the James kids seemed unable to make the transition to fully responsible adults—not surprising, perhaps, given their young ages and Gloria's enormous responsibilities. They tried to stay together in the house Freda had run with an iron fist and loving heart, but they knew nothing about maintenance. The house was already old and in poor condition when Freda died. As pipes began leaking, holes formed in the roof, and appliances failed, everyone knew they couldn't keep it up for very long. Finally they were forced to move, the house was condemned, and the James home was torn apart.

Terry and Curt left to fend for themselves. Gloria and Eddie were no longer dating, so Eddie left to live with his aunt. Though they all still would keep in touch, Gloria and LeBron were now alone, facing life on the streets. Even a move to the projects would have been a giant step up in the world.

ON THE MOVE

"After living on Hickory, we thought Elizabeth Park was the Taj Mahal," Gloria James said.

Elizabeth Park was a housing complex past its prime. To motorists looking down on the projects from the nearby Route 8 bridge, the brick row houses seemed to stretch forever. All the buildings looked the same; only the clothing hung to dry on lines strung about the complex gave some variety, telling a story about how many children might be in a family, what their favorite sports teams were. There were sections of open space where the children could play and where adults could gather. Everyone's backyard was everyone else's.

Elizabeth Park was a place to warehouse low-income black residents of all ages and backgrounds. Worse, the presence of alcohol and drugs was evident in the night music of screaming sirens, speeding police cars, and wailing family members as ambulances came for the victims of drunks, domestic violence, drive-by shootings, and gang fights.

Many residents were single mothers doing nothing or single mothers working hard to improve their lives and the lives of their children. There were also elderly residents who remembered when Elizabeth Park was an upstanding area to raise children, who knew that living in the projects didn't mean you couldn't be proud of your home.

Hazel Morton was one of those long-time residents. At the time Gloria and LeBron first came to the complex, she had spent more than 30 years in Elizabeth Park, not only as a resident but also serving on the executive board of the Akron Metropolitan Housing Authority. She knew the hazards, but she also remembered when the residents tried to pull together for the betterment of each other.

After Hazel Morton's husband passed away, she lived in Elizabeth Park as the single mother of five children, a situation that enabled her to relate to Gloria James, whose mother she had known. Hazel Morton was a widow and Gloria had never been married, but both were determined to succeed, to create the foundation for a better life for their children, and each would become a success in ways outsiders thought was impossible.

One of Morton's sons played professional football for the Buffalo Bills and then became a lawyer; his wife was a dentist. Another son was a career soldier in the Army National Guard. A third was a manager in the rubber industry in Akron, and the fourth also had a steady job. Hazel's daughter was a stay-at-home mother while her own children were young.

Morton's children had known the good life in the Elizabeth Park that changed dramatically by the time Gloria and LeBron moved there. It was a proud neighborhood in the early days.

"After my husband died, I preached to my kids that you could make a good living, make good grades, and make a good name for yourself even if you lived in the projects. You don't have to be a bad person and do bad things because you lived in the projects. A lot of people think because you live in the projects, you can't make it. You can, if you try, but you have to make an effort," said Morton.

"I never worried about the neighborhood when I was raising my kids, but it has gotten worse since my kids left," she said. "You have these young boys standing on the corner drinking . . . and not doing anything productive. They should get a job, even if it's at McDonald's making hamburgers or washing dishes. There's no shame in that. I tell people to this day, I'm proud to live in the projects and I'm grateful the housing authority let me live here this long."

Gloria and LeBron were never officially in residence in Elizabeth Park, but they lived there, on and off, for six years. It was their first stop on a semi-nomadic existence that would last until LeBron was 12.

After leaving the house on Hickory, Gloria and LeBron, now four and a half years old, headed for nearby Elizabeth Park because they knew people there—friends of Freda's, and schoolmates of Gloria or her brothers—who would take them in for a little while.

They shared space with other families, always moving around. Yet to Gloria, just having a portion of a suite in Elizabeth Park was wonderful. There were small but adequate play areas for the children, and there were many people like Hazel Morton. LeBron had an instant extended family—people who watched and worked to keep him out of trouble.

"I never had a minute's trouble with LeBron, and I never heard anything about him getting into any trouble the whole time he was here, either," Morton said. "I'm proud of Gloria and I'm proud of LeBron. He's 100 percent my guy."

Still, Elizabeth Park was a tough place to grow up, and it wasn't unusual to hear about violent crime happening nearby. For example, one day a section of the complex was cordoned off while 30 members of the Akron Police Special Weapons and

Tactics unit spent three and a half hours in a standoff with an armed man who had gotten into an argument with his neighbor, pulled a gun, and shot him.

"Anybody who knows about Elizabeth Park knows how bad it is," LeBron said. "You had gunshots flying and cop cars driving around there all the time. As a young boy, it was scary but I never got into none of that stuff. That just wasn't me. . . . I knew it was wrong."

LeBron grew up never really having anything. Nothing tangible, anyway—no nice home, no nice toys. All he had was Gloria. It could have been very easy for LeBron to give in to the pressures and temptations common to young boys in the projects.

Perhaps it was because LeBron felt emotionally secure in the love and nurturing of his mother and the extended family Gloria had surrounded him with that he didn't seek the approval of the older kids, the troubled youths who used the younger boys to help them participate in illegal activities.

LeBron was more secure in his own world. He was comfortable being alone, comfortable being with other boys only when they were involved in sports together. He avoided trouble wherever he could, though it was easier in some places than in others.

Gloria and LeBron continued to bounce around among friends—in Elizabeth Park and elsewhere.

Another friend was Bruce Kelker, a man about the same age as Gloria's older brother, Terry. He had known Freda and had seen the family decline after her death, seen their battle to insulate LeBron from all the negatives. Knowing that Gloria and LeBron always needed another place to stay, with each helping family assisting for only a few weeks or months as they could—

he offered space in his home in another part of Akron for whenever they needed.

Kelker was like many of the people Gloria sought during her years of need. She knew his character, knew she could trust his stability, and in Bruce's case knew he had been preapproved by her late mother, who enjoyed having him in her home in the years before and immediately after LeBron was born.

Kelker and Gloria didn't date; they were friends. Kelker had plenty of room in his home for Gloria and LeBron, and he could give them a couple of bedrooms and a bath. It was a simple way to help two people he cared about. He did what Freda had done for Eddie Jackson. It was an unusual arrangement, but it seemed to work. Kelker adored LeBron, and when Gloria wanted to date, the men she dated understood that there was nothing improper going on in the home. She and her son had a friend, an occasional sitter, and a helper through the rough times.

The only person who didn't understand was Kelker's girlfriend of the previous 14 years. Eventually she ordered him to choose between her and Gloria. Kelker tried to explain that he was just giving friends a place to stay, how much LeBron meant to him, how he would do anything to help the boy through the rough times, but the girlfriend wouldn't listen. Finally she gave Kelker an ultimatum: she would leave his life if he didn't get rid of Gloria. Kelker, like a championship poker player, never blinked. Gloria and LeBron stayed. There would only be a few more years during which he could have any influence in LeBron's life. He wasn't going to throw it away because of someone else's jealousy, no matter how much her loss hurt him.

But Gloria and LeBron kept moving around, to other friends, to other homes in the area. Always they were welcome and, more important, welcome to return. Always, though, they seemed destined for yet another move, another adjustment.

"When I was five, some financial things happened, and I moved seven times in a year," LeBron said in an interview with *ESPN The Magazine*. "My mom would always say, 'Don't get comfortable, because we may not be here long.'"

Gloria was getting into trouble occasionally, as is evident from the court records in Akron. There were several citations, minor offenses such as disorderly conduct, playing music too loudly, criminal trespassing, and contempt of court—behavior perhaps more juvenile than criminal. But Gloria was no longer a kid.

LeBron was certainly being affected by his unstable environment. School, for example, wasn't nearly as important to him as playing video games.

"In fourth grade, I missed 82 days of school out of 160," he said.

Yet LeBron stayed out of trouble. Instead he spent time walking from the apartment in which they were living to the corner store, or staying inside to play games. He was part loner and part lost, and neither the school staff nor others in his life seemed to make an extra effort to reach him, to bring him back into the classroom. Other boys his age were on the streets, experimenting with drugs, and being used as burglars by gangs of older kids who knew that someone his age would never do hard time. LeBron avoided all of that, and in doing so he never really entered the social service system.

FOUR

ORGANIZED SPORTS

LeBron might never have known real stability in his life if it weren't for organized sports, through which he would make several crucial personal connections that helped him evolve from troubled child into a remarkably focused teen.

LeBron first became involved with Pee Wee football through Bruce Kelker, who had himself played for Akron's South Rangers Pee Wee team as a youth. Kelker had become a responsible adult in part, he believed, because of what he learned as a kid on the football field instead of on the streets. He returned as an adult to be a volunteer coach for other children, including LeBron.

"LeBron had done nothing but play street ball. He had never played organized ball, and when we got him on the field, I'll tell you, I had never coached a kid who picked up the knowledge of the game so quick," Kelker said

During LeBron's first year of organized ball, playing with the South Rangers when he was nine, he scored 18 touchdowns in six games as a tailback. LeBron started out as a running back, but he was truly best as a receiver. "Even to this day, LeBron's power is in his hands," Kelker said.

The South Rangers were like a family, year 'round. Everyone involved with the organization cared about each other, not just during the football season, but even after the season was over. That was important to LeBron, who clearly felt a need for family.

"The South Rangers meant a lot to me," LeBron said. "All the coaches and the parents really cared about us, and they made playing the game fun. I actually wanted to play in the NFL because of my experience playing for the Rangers."

One of those coaches and parents, a former South Ranger himself, would soon became one of LeBron's strongest role models—and his first real basketball coach.

Every neighborhood has a guy like Frankie Walker, Sr. The guy who worked hard for his family but treated every kid like his own. The guy who made sure there were nets on the playground rim and that glass was swept off the court. The guy who volunteered to coach the youth basketball and football teams because he felt it was his duty to give young kids a strong role model. There were people like Walker during his own childhood who had made a difference in his life, so he was going to make sure he did the same thing—not only for his own kids but for all the kids in the community.

"I played for the South Rangers, and just learning about all the discipline, teamwork, and everything else it took, it made me what I am today," Walker said.

Frankie Walker was the type of man who cared more about the welfare of the boys on his team than if they won or lost their games.

Frankie worked for the Akron Metropolitan Housing Authority (AMHA), and his wife worked for Congressman Tom Sawyer for the 15 years before he was defeated for reelection. Then she worked for Congressman Sherrod Brown. They lived on the west side of the city in a middle-class neighborhood.

However, Frankie and Pam understood people like Gloria James and the struggle of raising children with little money, because the Walkers had struggled at times, as well.

As they got to know Gloria, Frankie and Pam recognized that she was a boisterous, aggressive, and opinionated woman who sometimes made friendship difficult. At the same time, they saw how dedicated she was to her son. So when LeBron did not immediately return to his fourth grade classes following the Christmas break from school, they became concerned. Frankie talked with other parents who knew Gloria and her son better than he did. He wanted to find out what was wrong without embarrassing Gloria.

Frankie soon learned that this was one of those troubled times for the James family. Gloria needed time away from LeBron to get her own life together rather than continuing to run from crisis to crisis. Frankie talked with his wife, Pam, his daughters, Chanelle and Tanesha, and his son, Frankie, Jr. The family decided to offer LeBron a temporary home in order to give Gloria the time and space she needed. This would not be a foster arrangement; it would not be a situation where Gloria was denied access to her son; it would solely be a case where each was sleeping in a different home at night, but the two would be together as often as Gloria wanted. They would spend each weekend together.

The arrangement the Walkers offered was a familiar one, based on the same sort of compassion Freda James had shown in her neighborhood. There was nothing condescending or judgmental about it. Gloria accepted.

"It was like a new beginning for me," LeBron said later. "When I moved in with the Walkers, I went from missing 87 days my fourth-grade year to zero days in the fifth grade. They all may not know how much I care about them, but I care about them a lot. I love them. They are like my family, too, and I wouldn't be here without them."

LeBron thrived in the new environment, though he was first startled by the change. Gloria's immaturity and the tremendous stresses she was under meant there had been little consistency in LeBron's day. Gloria watched the *Tonight Show* before going to bed each night, and LeBron, who still had to get up for school, had watched at her side.

It was quite different at the Walkers.

"They showed me discipline. So that was a huge step, even though I know when I woke up in the morning, I never wanted to go to school. I didn't want to go. Mrs. Walker would wake me up at 6:15; we had to be to school by 8:00.

The Walkers insisted that LeBron share the discipline of their three children. He had to take his turn cleaning the bathroom, and he had to pick up after himself. He had a regular schedule for homework and bedtime. He went to school every day, taking pride in achieving a perfect attendance record his fifth grade year. And he spent every weekend with his mother, as well as whatever other time was possible.

The Walkers came to look upon LeBron as a member of their extended family, creating birthday and Christmas rituals for LeBron and Gloria. They encouraged Gloria when she tried to make a permanent go of reuniting with LeBron during his sixth grade year, but he continued to be shuttled back and forth when Gloria's finances did not allow her a permanent residence.

Sports continued to offer LeBron much-needed structure in his life—and they continued to expand his extended family. This time, the sport was basketball. The game soon brought

LeBron together with several other coaches and youths who would become the best of friends, and it quickly revealed some of the most important traits of LeBron's developing personality.

Frankie Walker coached organized basketball in a recreation league at the Summit Lake Community Center, an inner-city rec center where many black kids went to learn the game from dedicated amateur coaches. On one wall of the center was a mural honoring Akron's own Gus Johnson, a former NBA star. On the court, some of the top grade-school kids battled it out—among them Walker's son, Frankie Jr.

One day when LeBron was ten years old, Frankie Sr. took the two boys to the playground to play ball. Frankie Jr., though smaller than LeBron, was a much more developed player because his dad had been coaching him for years already. LeBron just had raw talent. One on one, LeBron lost badly. Frankie Sr. remembered with a mix of bemusement and pride that his son "whupped LeBron something like 21 to 7." LeBron was crushed, hating the defeat, hating the game, and realizing that there was more to playing it than shooting a ball towards a hoop.

The coach wasn't trying to embarrass LeBron. He put his arm around the boy and told him he would teach him how to not only play the game, but to understand it. He kept his promise, and about a month later LeBron, who normally shot right-handed, was putting up left-handed layups.

When LeBron joined Walker's recreation league, Walker had plenty of opportunity to teach LeBron—and watch his remarkably rapid development.

LeBron wasn't particularly skilled at first, but each time he was shown a new move—a better way to control the ball or shoot or play defense—he got it.

"I had never coached a kid who picked things up and excelled in them as quickly as LeBron," Frankie Walker, Sr. said. "He doesn't golf, but if he picked up some golf clubs, Tiger Woods better watch out."

LeBron was an intense competitor right from the start. Bruce Kelker, having noticed that LeBron was a natural athlete, tried to interest him in other sports. The one game that LeBron refused to continue playing, though, was baseball.

"He was good in baseball, too," said Kelker, "but when he was like in the fourth or fifth grade, the team he played for his first year lost their first three games and he couldn't handle it, so he quit." It was the only time Kelker saw LeBron quit anything related to athletics.

Frankie Walker, Sr. noticed the young athlete's competitive streak, but he was more impressed with his sportsmanship.

"LeBron hated to lose," said Walker, "but he wasn't a poor sport and he didn't pout. If he lost, he would just practice so that the next time, he didn't lose."

But what really made LeBron stand out from the other kids playing the game, Walker noted, was how quickly he learned to *think* basketball. He began to approach the game of basketball the way a chess master approaches chess.

Most kids learn the game of basketball by practicing shots from different spots on the floor and then playing against good competition. They learn ball handling on the court and under the pressure of other players trying to take the ball from them. They learn to play one or more positions. The basics can make for an outstanding player and a successful team.

Great players, though, also train their minds.

In chess, the idea is to think several moves ahead. In basketball, LeBron had the ability to see ahead. It was as though, in his mind, he would slow the game and mentally cut through the tricks, the "moves," the feints, and the other ways players try to trick each other out. LeBron learned to see not only what the offense was doing but also the way the defense would come at him and his teammates. He learned to read where the ball was going and to make a defensive adjustment even as the opposing players were just getting into position themselves.

Frankie Walker, Sr. was surprised by what LeBron had learned on the team during his fourth-grade year and impressed with the leadership skills he already showed. So impressed, in fact, that during LeBron's fifth-grade year he made LeBron an assistant coach of the fourth-grade team, arranging practice sessions so that LeBron could continue playing with his fifth-grade team.

"I didn't think anything of it because LeBron was so [much more] mature than most of the kids, especially when it came to knowing about the game," Frankie Walker, Sr. said. "He was just one of those kids who knew the X's and O's."

FIVE

SPRING HILL

When Gloria and LeBron finally found a permanent home together in 1995—the first they shared in six years—they rejoiced. A two-bedroom, rent-assisted suite in the Spring Hill Apartments was, for 11-year-old LeBron and his mom, the greatest happiness they could imagine. Gloria took the smaller bedroom so that her growing boy could have more space for himself. True, the neighborhood, like Elizabeth Park, was held in disdain. But that little mattered; it was *home*. They would be settled there for the next seven years.

LeBron was enrolled in the sixth grade at Riedinger Middle School for the 1995–1996 school year. Joe Caito was principal, and he was used to dealing with kids from nontraditional families. He also was familiar with the James family.

"I knew Gloria and her mother," said Caito. "When Gloria was an eighth grader, I had her for a year in two classes and she did extremely well. I also knew she changed [getting a little wild] once she got to high school, but during my experiences with her and LeBron, they showed no signs of being a dysfunctional family."

LeBron's reputation as a good athlete preceded him at Riedinger Middle School, though he was not known as a basketball player; rather it was thought he would probably excel in football. But it was as a student that LeBron began to blossom at Riedinger.

During elementary school, LeBron had been an indifferent student. "Before all of this sports thing got started, like when I was in the fourth grade, I would just play video games like all little boys do," LeBron said. "School wasn't that important to me, and I really didn't care about anything except playing video games or basketball."

But by middle school, thanks in large part to the influence of the Walker family, his attitude had changed. He knew he couldn't succeed without doing the work.

He didn't like to go to class and see everyone else turning in homework when his wasn't done. "It gets to me. I really didn't like doing homework, but when you know you'll be the only one not turning it in, it doesn't feel right," LeBron said. "I have a lot of pride. I just want to give the best I can. I'm not going to try to tell someone to try to get straight A's, and I'm not going to tell my kids to get straight A's because that's too much pressure on a kid. I'm going to tell them to do their best. Being a straight-A student is a gift. Straight-A students do the same as we do but they are A students and the rest of us are B students. The straight-A student can do everything better because it just comes natural. I'm an A student in basketball. We are blessed with the gifts that God gave us and it's important to use your gifts the right way."

Acting as assistant coach in fifth grade gave LeBron his understanding of what it meant to be a role model. He was so close in age to the fourth graders that they wanted to be just like him. He realized that whatever he did, both in the gym and in the classroom, would be seen as important. He understood that his attitude towards school would be their attitude towards school. He believed working hard in the classroom was the right thing to do. He just didn't want to do it. With all the boys on the younger team watching, though, he began doing what he felt was right, not just what he wanted to do.

LeBron knew he was gifted as an athlete. He had no idea how far he might go. But he noticed that he learned faster and played better than boys who were older and more experienced. He didn't realize how smart he was until he began making the merit roll and honor roll in school. This meant either a 3.0 to 3.49 average for the merit roll, and 3.5 or higher for the honor roll. Had he not been the type of boy who could count on a sports scholarship, he easily would have earned a scholarship based on proven academics.

LeBron had top grades during his seventh and eighth grade years. "LeBron was very serious about his grades," said Caito. "He was just a model student. He was never in the principal's office for discipline reasons."

Caito did recall a time when he caught LeBron where he wasn't supposed to be. Sixth graders ate lunch before the seventh and eighth graders at Riedinger; after the kids ate lunch, they were allowed to go into the gym to play basketball until the lunch period was over. LeBron finished his lunch one day but decided later to go back to the eighth grade lunch period. Caito looked in the gym and saw LeBron schooling the eighth graders. Caito didn't want to bust LeBron just yet; he kept hidden behind the door, watching sixth-grader outplay kids two years older. Finally, Caito opened the door and motioned to LeBron. "I said, 'Are you supposed to be in here?' He said, 'No sir.' Then I said, 'OK. I don't want to see you in there again.'" LeBron learned his lesson and walked away. Caito turned his head and said, "Oh my goodness, that kid is going to be a great basketball player."

LeBron wasn't just working harder at getting good grades to please the principal, though, as an incident from his high school years showed.

Layman Bowick got to know LeBron and Gloria as neighbors. Bowick, a proud, hard-working man with a kind heart, had lived in Spring Hill for 25 years, living with his wife and watching children be born and raised to adulthood. He often visited with Gloria and LeBron, just to shoot the breeze and see what was going on in their lives. Even when LeBron began to get special recognition for his basketball skill in high school, to Bowick he was just another youth in need of guidance and love.

"I loved Gloria and LeBron, and LeBron knew I wouldn't kiss his booty just because he played basketball," Bowick said. "I'm a grown man and I'll give everybody respect, no matter how old they are, as long as they give me respect, and LeBron always gave me respect. That's why I love that kid. And I love Gloria for raising such a respectful kid."

Bowick discovered a small secret about LeBron.

He happened to be visiting Gloria and LeBron's apartment one time when he stopped in the boy's bedroom to say hello and noticed LeBron going over some books and papers.

"What you doing, boy?" he asked.

"Oh," LeBron said. "I'm just doing my homework."

Bowick glanced around the room. He had seen the countless sports honors—medals, banners, citations—cluttering the walls before. But this time he noticed a slightly tattered and yellowed certificate hanging on the wall. It looked like one of those artificially aged copies of the Declaration of Independence you might see in a souvenir shop.

The piece of paper was a citizenship award from LeBron's seventh-grade year at Riedinger.

"I can still remember that," said Joe Caito. "I remember how proud he was after he won that award. It didn't surprise me at all that he still had it."

AAU

LeBron began playing in Amateur Athletic Union (AAU) basketball competition in fifth grade, after the Summit Lake Rec League season ended. It was there that the core of a high school basketball phenomenon began to develop.

The team LeBron played for was called the Shooting Stars, and they were outstanding. Chris Marciniak started the program, setting up coaching clinics and team camps, but it was one of his customers, Dru Joyce, who brought together the foursome that became best friends as well as extraordinarily successful teammates.

Dru brought his two sons to the camps. His older son, "Little Dru" Joyce, and his friend Sian Cotton joined LeBron as teammates. Theirs became a classic tale of kids who become friends at a young age and then never let anything get in the way of that friendship.

Little Dru was the quiet kid who had a mouth. Even when he was a freshman in high school, he was only 5'-6" and his game shorts hung so low they looked like sweat pants. When Dru walked on the court, he looked like the ball boy—but he could kill you with his accurate outside shooting.

Sian was the clown of the bunch. He was always bigger than

the rest of the guys—in a too-many-Hostess-cupcakes kind of way—but was an exceptional athlete for his size.

The fourth, who would join them a few years later, was initially their opponent in AAU ball.

LeBron, Dru, and Sian would say that when they were playing AAU ball together, Willie McGee was one of the best of the bunch.

"We were in a couple of [AAU] tournaments and when we played against Willie, we were like, 'man, we can use him on our team,'" Sian said. "He was a guard and he could handle the rock. We had to get him."

He would also turn out to be an important personal influence on LeBron.

Willie McGee was the kind of kid you'd want your daughter to marry. Polite, mild-mannered, intelligent, and ambitious.

When you talked to Willie, you just got the impression that he would eventually do something big after high school, like become president of a successful company, or run for public office. That's why Willie was called the mature one of the bunch, because he always seemed to be in control, for the most part, and always seemed older than he was.

There was a reason why Willie had to grow up so quick. Like LeBron, he was without a biological father in the home and from a background that could have left him a stereotyped inner-city kid involved with gangs, drugs, and other self-destructive behavior.

The McGees lived in Chicago as an extended family. Willie's grandmother helped his mother with her three children. Illya McGee, Willie's older brother, a star high school basketball player in Chicago, was offered the chance to play as a freshman at the University of Akron.

Willie was still in elementary school when Illya moved to

Akron, and to Willie, losing Illya—as close to being a father as anyone in his life—was similar to abandonment.

"I didn't have that male influence in my life when Illya left, so I was missing a lot of school and I just wasn't doing well in school," said Willie. "I don't mean to say anything bad about my mother, grandmother, and sister, but when you don't have a male role model in your life, it's hard."

Willie often visited his brother in Akron during the basketball season, and during Illya's senior year he agreed with his mother and grandmother that Willie should move to Akron and live with him. For a young man on the verge of starting his own life, it was a tough decision. Yet as someone who wanted to enter social work, he knew that taking in his younger brother was also the only way to save him from an increasingly self-destructive life back in Chicago.

"Moving to Akron was different," Willie said. "I got away with a lot of stuff when Illya was gone and I was still in Chicago, but when I moved to Akron, it was more strict, and I needed that. I stayed with my brother and sister-in-law. They were living on campus and I didn't have any kids to play with, but they exposed me to a lot of little things, like going to the movies, going out to dinner, plus I got to watch Illya play basketball so it was a thrill for me and I changed my life around."

Willie began playing AAU basketball on a team that played against Coach Dru's Shooting Stars. The boys who played in the league were considered the top athletes in their respective grades, and they were closely watched. In AAU ball, the coaches came to you. They would let you know if you were good enough to play on *their* team. Teams would compete against teams in their area, their region, their state, and, if they were good enough, against the best from other states. During the course of the AAU season, LeBron's team would often see Willie's team playing, and they were impressed with Willie's ability. "I liked how Willie played and I knew we could use him," LeBron said.

Loyalty was important to Willie, though, and he didn't feel right about leaving his own team to join the other. "They saw me and wanted me to play, but I felt I couldn't leave my team because I was the best on our squad and I just couldn't leave them like that," Willie said.

But Willie's coach understood that his best player would become a better player if he was challenged by working with LeBron, Little Dru, and Sian. He encouraged Willie to switch teams, a move that Willie found to be bittersweet. "I hated to leave my friends," he said. However, he quickly realized that he had the same drive, the same spirit, and the same sense of loyalty as the stars of his new team. "When I started with 'Bron' and those guys, it just clicked right from the start."

Clicked is perhaps an understatement. In five years of AAU competition, this group won six national championships. And that would be just the beginning of their basketball career.

AAU competition was the first time most of these boys experienced the reality of basketball as a national sport. AAU competition was ultimately nationwide, the top teams coming together for a tournament once a year.

"I'll never forget the first time we made it to the AAU national tournament when the kids were 11 and 12," Coach Dru told *The Plain Dealer* in an interview. "The tournament was in Salt Lake City, and it was the first time most of the kids had ever been on a plane, including LeBron. He cried from Hopkins all the way to Houston."

In August of 1997, the Shooting Stars won the 12-and-under division of the Youth Basketball of America National Tournament in Orlando, Florida. They competed against 31 teams from 20 states and Puerto Rico. In the 65-47 championship win against the Charlotte Stars, LeBron scored 13 points, Sian scored 12, and Little Dru had 10 points. LeBron was named the Most Valuable Player of the tournament, while Sian and Dru made the all-tournament team. The Shooting Stars also competed in the AAU national tournament at Salt Lake City that same year and finished 10th in a 71-team field.

The next year, the Shooting Stars won another championship at the Youth Basketball of America National Tournament held in Orlando. The players were 13 and under and defeated the Kenner Eagles of New Orleans 53-36 in the championship. In that game, LeBron scored 21 points and Sian was named MVP of the tournament.

For the guys, traveling together was all about becoming closer as friends. They would stay up until 5 a.m. the morning of a game, play at 10 a.m., and still win. "We would just giggle and laugh all night," Sian said.

It was all about developing and solidifying new friendships. "When I went to nationals with all the guys, it was important," Willie said. "I really didn't know them, but Coach Dru really made a good impression on my brother, so [Illya] trusted them enough to let me travel with them. When we went to Florida, that's when I really started getting close to all of them."

"We didn't know Willie that well," Sian said, "but he was quiet and we never had any problems with him. When he got on the court, he always gave us a spark. He was always getting the loose rebounds, he played good defense, he could shoot, he had it all. I agree that the trip to nationals in Florida was an important year for all of us in a lot of ways."

"They believed in themselves and each other because they have played in all kinds of different situations," Coach Dru said. "They've been like that since they were 10 and 11."

Coach Dru knew he had special players who were extremely talented and unselfish, and that's the only way he'd have it. "When LeBron was playing in the Summit Lake Rec League, he would score most of his team's points," Coach Dru said. "When I got him, the first thing I taught him was that on my team, there were no prima donnas. Not that he had that attitude; I just explained to him that everyone was equal and you had to play as a team."

Coach Dru considered Little Dru a better player than Sian, Willie, and even LeBron when they were 10 and 11.

"I'm not just saying this because Dru is my son, but Dru was the better player out of all of them," he said. "You knew LeBron had tons of potential and that he had outstanding ability. He was more of a natural athlete and when he played for us, he fit right in."

Coach Dru remembers picking LeBron up from a rec league game to take him to a local AAU game. "We were driving down East Avenue and I told LeBron, "We all know you can score. But what I want you to do with us is get your points in the flow of the game. Don't try to do too much, just get everybody involved in the game and let the game come to you.'"

For LeBron, playing on the Shooting Stars was all about winning, and the teammates expected nothing less. The fun came when they won, so they became addicted to victory and the high that came with it.

"Some people say when you're younger and you were playing basketball that it was okay to lose," LeBron said. "None of us were like that. We didn't want to lose at all. None of us were losers. We were raised that you gotta win, it was just survival. But it was *always* fun. It was never *not* fun."

The AAU practices were set up where the players would have to battle each other in drills. It made each player better. It made the team better, when you had everyone playing to the best of his ability and having LeBron pushing you all the way.

"LeBron got to where he was because of the struggles he's been through," Willie said. "We helped LeBron along the way just like he helped us. But his talent was there right from the start."

LeBron and his friends had a fabulous AAU career, winning more than 200 games. However, they also came to understand that winning at one level of competition makes you a target for the next. They were at the top of elementary and middle school competition now; they were ready to take on high school.

COACH DAMBROT

LeBron's life had already been filled with men and women in transition, the lost and damaged connecting with those who had become stable enough to reach out to others in need of a helping hand. Eddie Jackson had found Freda James. Gloria and LeBron had found Bruce Kelker, the Walkers, and so many others who showed them kindness.

Now, on the brink of the transition to high school, LeBron would cross paths with someone else trying to rebuild a life. It would have a great impact on both their futures.

Keith Dambrot's own journey had taken him to within sight of coaching greatness, then plunged him into disgrace and exile from the game he loved.

As a college basketball coach, Dambrot had been on the fast track. He began his coaching career at Ashland (Ohio) University in 1989. He was head coach at Tiffin (Ohio) University, an assistant at Eastern Michigan and Akron University. By May 1991, Dambrot was already head coach at Division-I Central Michigan and only 32 years old.

And then he became embroiled in a racial controversy that took away his career.

During halftime of a heated game, Dambrot used the most hateful of racial epithets in a misguided attempt to stir up his players. He intended the word not to offend but to try to connect with his players, most of whom were black, on a gut level, using the jargon they used themselves. Not only did the speech fail miserably on the court (his team was trounced), it quickly stirred up a whirlwind of trouble for the coach.

Dambrot was suspended without pay for four days. And when word of the coach's comments began to circulate across campus in the days that followed, his firing was inevitable. The remark was too shocking. The sports sections of newspapers throughout the United States headlined the incident. Various magazines and sports television shows mentioned what he said. The Reverend Jesse Jackson brought his Rainbow Coalition into the fray.

"It was naïve and unprofessional," Dambrot explained. "I asked permission to use the word. I said we had to be tougher, more hard, more aggressive and I used the word. It was stupid on my part, but everyone present understood the context in which the term was used, and no one in our locker room who heard me was offended or complained."

Dambrot knew he had screwed up, but he was emotionally shattered by also being called a racist. "I know I hurt people by what I said, but it really, really hurt me that I was being called a racist."

Dambrot had been raised by Jewish parents not only known to be liberals but who, according to family friends, had taught their son to be accepting of all people, regardless of their economic status, race, or ethnic background. His mother, Faye Dambrot, had started the women's studies program at the University of Akron and was a strong, vocal proponent of equal rights.

"When I got fired from Central Michigan, it was really hard for my mom because she knew what I stood for and what our family stood for," Dambrot said.

Forced from the career he loved, Dambrot returned home to Akron and became a very successful stockbroker, providing a good living for his family and keeping a low profile. As several years passed, he stayed out of coaching—but not by choice; he just couldn't get hired. No school wanted to go through the media scrutiny of hiring a coach once accused of being a racist.

Despite the rejections, he just couldn't stay away from the game. He had to be in a gym. It was killing him not to be where the balls were bouncing.

Keith Dambrot's resurrection in basketball came through the Jewish Community Center, a facility that was open to all neighborhood kids. Dambrot, a member of the center, began running Sunday basketball clinics there. Nothing fancy or intense; just a place where kids of all races who were serious about wanting to improve their skills could go to learn fundamentals. Dambrot charged each kid a dollar.

One summer, as Dambrot was conducting a clinic, he noticed a young kid working his butt off. This kid had impressive skills: he was an exceptional dribbler, he could shoot from the outside, and he seemed to have great knowledge of the game. It was Dru Joyce III. Dambrot quickly took a liking to Little Dru. There was something about Dru that reminded Dambrot of himself. Maybe it was the fact that Dambrot had been just as short as Dru was when he was that age—and the fact that Dru loved to play basketball—anytime, anywhere.

"When I met Little Dru, he was in the eighth grade and he was a gym rat," said Dambrot. Dru spent all his free time there practicing.

Pretty soon word got out that this guy, Dambrot, was a really nice guy who seemed to love kids and basketball. Dambrot's clinics started to grow from a couple dozen to 120. Then, Dru brought started bringing other kids with him—Sian, Willie, and LeBron. The four attended Dambrot's clinics almost every Sunday during their eighth grade year.

The clinics were some satisfaction, but Dambrot wanted a return to real coaching—he wanted a team, and he was still looking for a school that wanted him.

There were openings at two local public schools—including his alma mater, Firestone High. Neither school would hire him. The only other opening in town was a low-paying job at a small Catholic school: St. Vincent-St. Mary High School. Dambrot wanted any coaching job. Salary didn't matter, and having a winning team didn't matter if the best he could put on the court was not as good as the competition.

"All I knew is that I wanted it and just had to get back into coaching because I loved the kids and I loved the game, but more than anything, I loved the kids," Dambrot said.

He was interviewed, approved, and in July of 1998, he became St. Vincent-St. Mary's varsity boys basketball coach.

Fred Ost, president of St. Vincent-St. Mary at the time, later said, "We hired Keith because we were looking for someone who knew basketball. He was a teacher of the game, and someone who could enforce discipline. For us, what happened to Keith [at Central Michigan] never entered into our judgment because I knew his mother and knew she certainly didn't raise a racist, so I wasn't worried at all about whether we would take abuse or not."

Dambrot was ecstatic to be back in coaching, finally. Someone had given him a second chance, and he would be forever grateful to the administration at St. Vincent-St. Mary. He was also grateful to the parents of the kids on the team, who raised no objections even though many were aware of his recent trouble. Some took a wait-and-see attitude. Some assumed he had learned his lesson or he would not have been hired. And some felt he was not the man he had been portrayed to be, especially those who had witnessed his words and actions when their sons attended his sessions at the Jewish Community Center.

Dambrot himself had no illusions about where he was and the opportunity he had been given. "I wasn't very hirable. I didn't hear anybody knocking my door down. I was truly thankful for those parents who gave me the opportunity to coach their kids."

Steve Culp, a white guy in his thirties and a native of the Boston area, could out-play any high school kid he encountered, or so he thought.

Culp was an assistant basketball coach at St. Vincent-St. Mary High School, which regularly opened its gym during the summer and fall to city kids for pickup basketball.

One day Culp and some older players decided to have a pickup game against LeBron and some others.

Culp watched the skinny young kid guarding him. "I put the ball out in front of LeBron," he said. "I waited for him to reach for it and I crossed it over. He slipped on his ass, then I went left and everyone started laughing at him because he was getting scored on by some old guy.

"So, now I'm coming back up the court and I'm thinking he'll do what most young kids do after something like that and go into a shell. But LeBron came right back at me, and I kind of started backing up on my heels. So I'm like, 'Damn, this kid is coming at me and wants to show me up.'"

LeBron missed his next shot, but someone on his team got the rebound and LeBron demanded the ball. It was a rare selfish display by LeBron. "In the eighth grade, LeBron had that competitive spirit that you don't even see in college guys," Culp said. The battle between the thirty-something Culp and the eighth grader went back and forth, two or three times up and down the court until the game ended. Culp was sold. "I've seen a lot of great young players, but I had never seen a young kid like that before," he said. "He had personality that you only see out of really experienced players . . . He just got more competitive as it went on, and that's when I went over to Coach Dambrot and said, 'This kid is going to be unreal.'"

Dambrot knew LeBron, of course, as well as Little Dru and the others from his Sunday clinics. And he certainly knew that they were now eighth-graders, about to enter high school. But he claims he didn't try to recruit them.

"As far as I figured, they were all going to Buchtel," he said.

Certainly the rumor was that the four—LeBron, Dru, Sian, and Wille—would attend predominantly-black Buchtel High School, one of the eight Akron public high schools on the west side of the city. And that made sense, given the fact that Dru lived just blocks from the school and his dad, Dru Joyce II, was an assistant coach on staff at Buchtel.

"But see, Little Dru was smart," said Dambrot. "Even though his dad was on the coaching staff there, he knew he could kind of get lost there. But I think Little Dru started to get to know me a little better and figured, 'If I got to play for this guy, I might get a shot to play.'"

Little Dru recognized that he was the type of player who might get overlooked. He was a relatively short kid, and no matter how hard he worked at the basics and being part of the team, there were always coaches who would pick the tallest boys in the hope that it would give them an edge in competition. However, he also knew that Coach Dambrot was concerned about the boys building character, gaining experience, and working to win—and was being focused solely on using the biggest, fastest, most aggressive players. With Dambrot he would not have to ride the bench because of his height. He would be truly part of a team, and that would mean being on the floor when they went against other schools.

Little Dru did decide he wanted to play for Dambrot at St. Vincent-St. Mary.

"Keith was the kind of guy we all wanted to play for," Dru said. "Our thing was we were all going to play together."

LeBron, Sian, and Willie shared Little Dru's respect for Coach Dambrot, and though they had the height and skills to be first string wherever they went, they followed the coach to St. Vincent-St. Mary.

And so the rest of the crew followed, holding to a pact they hade made during AAU competition: they would all go to the same high school together—to win a state championship.

EIGHT

FRESHMAN YEAR

St. Vincent-St. Mary became the unlikely vessel in which was prepared one of the most successful high school basketball teams in the nation. This was not a basketball school. It was not a sports school. It was a school meant to give teenagers a firm grounding in morals, ethics, and knowledge needed for college and for life. For example, in addition to optional electives in the freshman year, incoming students took Religious Education, English, Mathematics, Science, World History, Plan For Success, Physical Education, Health, and, if they were in a college prep program, a foreign language.

Each course was assigned from one-quarter credit to a full credit. English received a full credit for the students. Mathematics received a full credit. Religious Education received a full credit. Physical Education was only a quarter-credit course. So unimportant was what once was called "gym class" to the school administration that by the junior year it was no longer a requirement. Students might join one of the sports, and many did. But the focus of St. Vincent-St. Mary's was always the academic side of life. In 2003, 95% of the school's seniors went on to attend college.

(In fact, when the class of 2003 graduated, each student's name was listed in the program along with the place they would go the following year. Philip R. Alvord was going to Wilmington College; Alexander K. Aupperle to the University of Akron; and so on through LeBron James, National Basketball Association. Nothing distinguished LeBron, who by then was about to become the richest rookie player in the NBA, from Philip R. Alvord, alphabetically leading the list, except for an asterisk by Alvord's name, calling special attention to the fact that he was a scholarship recipient. Academic achievement warranted extra notice.)

For LeBron, St. Vincent-St. Mary quickly became another part of his ever-growing extended family.

Already at the school—and on the basketball team—two years ahead of LeBron was one of his close childhood friends, Maverick Carter. (They were so close that they called each other cousins.) And now joining the coaching staff as volunteer assistants would be Dru Joyce III and Sian's father, Lee Cotton.

Both men became interested in working with Dambrot when they learned of their sons' interests. Some people criticized Dambrot for hiring the two, thinking that he had used them to persuade their kids to choose his school, but that wasn't the case.

"The kids had already decided that they were coming to St. V," Dambrot said. "Big Dru approached me and asked if he and Lee could coach. I'm thinking, heck, these guys have coached a lot of AAU games with these kids, and they're going to be coming to every game anyways, so I'd rather have them on my side."

There were also two paid assistant coaches for St. Vincent-St. Mary: former NBA player Charles Thomas (whose twin brother, Carl Thomas, had been a guard for the Cleveland Cavaliers) and Amy Sherry, a two-time Mid-American Conference Women's Player of the Year from Kent State (and one of the final cuts by the WNBA Cleveland Rockers in 1997). Dambrot didn't hire a black man and woman to make himself look good. He hired them because he knew them personally, knew that they were basketball people, and as Dambrot had always preached, basketball saws no colors. It was certainly an impressive coaching staff for a high school focused on academics.

It was important to LeBron—as well as to Dambrot—that both his mother and Eddie Jackson (who frequently attended LeBron's games) were willing to overlook Dambrot's past and give him their support. They didn't have to be so accepting.

Eddie and Gloria had come from backgrounds where many whites and even middle-class blacks had vilified, mocked, or ignored them. There were other high schools to choose from— good schools where most of the kids were black, where the coaching staff was mostly black, where LeBron would be in a situation they felt might be less likely to cause problems. Instead, they accepted a man who was white, Jewish, and had been kicked out of the college coaching circuit for using a racial epithet.

"Everybody says things and don't mean it, internally," Eddie said. "When I met Keith, I had a problem with what I had heard, but after talking to him, I knew he didn't say those things in a hateful manner. I can't see a racial bone in his body." And after watching Keith coach, Eddie liked his style. "Oh my goodness, Keith was the man. You had that Division-I college mentality coaching these kids. Keith had a look on his face and when he looked at the kids, they would straighten the hell up. Keith was a hell of a coach. He kept that fire in them."

Gloria said simply, "Keith is my man. He's alright."

In the small city atmosphere of Akron, an unusual phenomenon was beginning to develop at a parochial school not known for its athletic prowess, led by a coach tainted by controversy, driven by a tight-knit and intensely competitive group of friends with one extraordinarily talented central figure.

The St. Vincent-St. Mary Irish had been a good basketball team during Dambrot's first year as their coach. They went a highly respectable 16-9 and lost in the Division III regional finals. Then, the expectations began to grow.

In 1999, Dambrot knew he had an excellent bunch of players. Maverick Carter was returning for his senior year, and now he would be joined by the four fabulous friends: LeBron, Dru, Sian, and Willie.

Other players strengthened St. Vincent-St. Mary's team with remarkable diversity. Among the starting five were Chad Mraz, a white youth from the wealthy suburb of Revere. His parents, Jeff and Sharon Mraz, had been childhood sweethearts raised in the inner city. They made certain their son was raised without prejudice either for color or economic background. Their home was regularly used by the team as the Mraz family hosted the boys—win or lose.

Aly Samabaly, a foreign exchange student from Mali, was one of the guards. His parents were killed in a car accident when he was young, and his older sister raised him before he came to the United States. Samabaly was 6'-3" but played like a much bigger young man. (He later played at Duquesne University.)

And there was John Taylor, a 6'-4" senior leader and team captain who looked like Richie Cunningham from *Happy Days*.

But Dambrot realized early on that however good this team might be, LeBron was clearly something special. And, he felt, a special responsibility. With this kid, Dambrot had been blessed by the basketball gods. He had never felt so much pressure coaching a kid as he now felt coaching LeBron; he didn't want to make any mistakes with his development.

LeBron's game still had a few flaws that would have to be worked out as he adjusted to high school play. Because he was already about 6'-4" and 170 pounds as a freshman, stronger and taller than most teenagers, he was able to use his body to muscle his way to the basket—and this reliance on an intense drive left his jump shot inconsistent. He would have to practice that, because when the other boys reached their full height he wouldn't be able to simply dominate them with a more aggressive game.

But such flaws were minor compared to the package of skills LeBron quickly began to demonstrate on the high school court. Early in the season, particularly after a big game against Cleveland Benedictine, LeBron was beginning to stand out.

"LeBron reminded me of an athletic Magic Johnson," Dambrot said. "He could rebound, pass, and defend. Physically, I had no idea he would develop like he did, but I knew mentally he had it. My feeling was that if he wanted to be the best ever, he had the talent to be, as long as he worked hard."

Dambrot didn't rely solely on his own judgment. When he was assistant coach at Eastern Michigan, he had worked under Ben Braun. The two were friends, and Dambrot kept in touch when Braun went on to the University of California, where he was named the Pac-10 Coach of the Year his first year in the league and also led the Golden Bears to a 23-9 season, reaching the NCAA Sweet 16.

Dambrot wanted his old friend's opinion of the phenomenon that was LeBron.

"I said, 'Look, Ben, I might be wrong, and I don't think I am, but this guy is going to be the best guy I've ever seen.'"

Braun respected Dambrot's knowledge of the game but he had his doubts. Until, that is, he accepted Dambrot's invitation to come watch LeBron play. The first time Braun saw LeBron play, he knew he was watching someone special.

"That kid won't ever play in college," Braun said.

LeBron was already marked—a professional just waiting until high school graduation so he could face the draft.

The Irish rolled along during LeBron's freshman season, racking up victories.

"Those guys really knew how to win," Dambrot said. "We had a small team, I mean, Maverick was our center for crying out loud [he was only about 6'-4"], but that team had to play great defense because it wasn't a great offensive team. We were small, but as far as pure grit and from a defensive standpoint, it was one of the strongest teams I ever coached, even at the collegiate level. The makeup and knowledge of the game from that group was incredible."

Things were looking endlessly bright for Dambrot as he guided the team to an undefeated regular season record, 20-0. By the time the postseason playoffs rolled around, the consensus was that St. Vincent-St. Mary was the team to beat. You didn't have to be a rocket scientist to figure that out. All the Irish needed to do was remain focused, play like they had all season, and they would walk away with the Division III state title.

But just a day before St. Vincent-St. Mary's regional title game, the last game before the state final four, Dambrot's mother, Faye, passed away of lung cancer at the age of 65.

Though she and her family thought she had beaten the cancer 10 years earlier, and she was vibrant and seemed in good health, the illness had returned that winter.

During his mother's last few weeks, Dambrot was spending his time sleeping at the Cleveland Clinic and at the Hospice in

Akron. He'd wake up, go to work, go to practice, then go back and sit or sleep next to his mom. It was an emotionally tough time for Dambrot, and it also affected his players. The boys relied on their coach, and they had never thought much about mortality. They were young and healthy, so were their parents; death was still something that happened in other people's families. This time it was happening to someone they considered one of their own.

The pressure of so many emotions, of so many responsibilities, began to take its toll. Dambrot decided he didn't want to coach anymore. His dying mother thought otherwise. Faye recognized her son's true love. She saw that he was depressed from the intense stress and exhaustion of her becoming physically weaker each day. She didn't want decisions made at such time to be regretted later. She would not tolerate his giving up.

Dambrot said, "One thing that my mom always told me was, 'You've come this far and you owe these kids. No matter what happens to me, you owe those kids.'

"My mother loved all of those kids and they all went to see her when she was in Hospice," Dambrot said. "She loved it and she needed it and that's something I know she always remembered."

For her, this team was vindication for her son.

"The St. Vincent-St. Mary job was a reprieve for me and my family," Dambrot said. "It showed that we came back. That's what made my mother so proud, the fact that white kids and black kids gave us an opportunity to come back."

The team managed to stay focused, won the regional title game, and prepared to battle for the Division III state championship.

For Dambrot, who a year before had felt lucky to have any

team at all, it was like a dream to be taking such a special group of youngsters toward a championship. One big reason they were headed to Columbus was the remarkable growth of LeBron as a team leader that season.

LeBron had worked hard at improving his own skills.

"I was just lucky to coach a guy like him who would just listen to everything you said and tried to get better all the time," said Dambrot. "At the end of his freshman year, LeBron knew more about basketball then 90 percent of the college players I ever had. He had unbelievable knowledge of the game."

But even more important was the way LeBron was learning to play as a part of a *team*.

"He had a knack of making other players better," Dambrot said. "If you ever noticed that when he played bad teams, he always got other players involved. He has such a sense of security and self-confidence about him that most guys don't have. Most guys would go out and get 50 points against a bad team, but LeBron would go get 15 points against a bad team but would make sure everybody else was getting into the game. If he needed to, he could elevate his game."

In Columbus, Dambrot would see one of the finest individual performances by a player of that entire undefeated season. And it wasn't from LeBron.

In the Value City Arena at Ohio State University, 13,061 fans turned out to see St. Vincent-St. Mary play in the title game against Jamestown Greenview High School. LeBron James, the player everyone was starting to watch closely, did what was expected of him. He scored 25 points. But the big surprise came from Little Dru.

While LeBron already had the size of a basketball star, at 6'-4" tall and 170 pounds, 15-year-old Little Dru kept his nickname not just because of his father but because, at 5'-6" he was 10 inches shorter and about 50 pounds lighter than his friend and fellow freshman.

Little Dru came off the bench and proceeded to dominate the floor with three-pointers, nailing seven out of seven, just one shy of the state tournament record in Division III. His 21 points were four shy of LeBron's total, but the way in which he achieved them was spectacular.

"It was an amazing feeling," Dru said. "I never expected anything like this." Dru also did not expect the television cameras that surrounded him, the on-court interviews at the end of the game, and the way his teammates hoisted him into the air as the fans cheered and shouted "Druuuuuu!" He later said that he felt 10 feet tall.

The player who chose St. Vincent-St. Mary because he thought he'd get a chance to play there despite his size had shown the wisdom of that decision.

"I knew Dru was a player the first time I saw him," Dambrot said later. "Watching him have a game like that was just a great feeling. He's just like me. We were the guys who didn't get picked on the playground because of our height.

"He always worked hard. Everyone said I only played Dru because his dad was on my staff. That wasn't true at all. I played Dru because he was a good player. We had the last laugh."

LeBron was as thrilled for his friend as he had been for his own triumphs that year. And there were many. But the player selected by Cleveland's *Plain Dealer* as Player of the Year that year was St. Vincent-St. Mary's Maverick Carter.

Tim Rogers was one of the *Plain Dealer* writers responsible for making that selection. The writers had mostly ignored the

LeBron James goes over the top—a fitting symbol for the overwhelming hype surrounding his rise to stardom as a high school phenom. (Akron Beacon Journal, Phil Masturzo)

The alley where LeBron played basketball while growing up on Hickory Street. The telephone pole once had a milk crate nailed to it so the kids could shoot baskets. (Patty Burdon)

Even at age three, LeBron showed his basketball prowess. On Christmas Day 1987, he was not told of the family tragedy that had happen earlier that day so that he could enjoy a normal holiday.
(James family)

The always photogenic LeBron at age five. Note the basketball watch on his left wrist.
(Courtesy of Wanda Reeves)

The James Gang (left to right): Curt, LeBron, Gloria and Terry. They didn't have much, but they always had each other. (Courtesy of Wanda Reeves)

Some close friends of Gloria's believe that Roland Bivins (shown here in his senior year at Akron's Central-Hower High School), was LeBron's biological father. However, Bivins's tragic death at a young age left the question unanswered.
(Courtesy of Gloria Bivins)

Gloria and Eddie Jackson were always a team, and their main goal was to make sure LeBron was surrounded by people who shared their love for him. Here, Gloria and Eddie are distributing LeBron bookmarks to kids living in the Elizabeth Park housing projects.
(Akron Beacon Journal, Phil Masturzo)

AAU was LeBron's first experience playing organized basketball. Here he is in fourth grade with the Hornets, coached by Frankie Walker Sr. By fifth grade, LeBron was so knowledgeable about the game that Walker asked him to help coach the fourth grade team. (Patty Burdon)

LeBron pushes the ball up the court in a game during his freshman season, when the Irish went 27-0 and won the Division III state championship. (Patty Burdon)

After controversy drove him from an NCAA Division I coaching job, Keith Dambrot wound up back in Akron teaching neighborhood kids basketball out of a love for the game. It was a big break for LeBron, and for St. Vincent-St. Mary high school. During his three seasons at the school, Dambrot won two state titles.

(Akron Beacon Journal, Phil Masturzo)

With his jersey loosely hanging off of his scrawny body, LeBron takes a moment to gather himself in a game during his freshman year. (Patty Burdon)

As freshmen, LeBron and his teammates got pumped up for a game by dancing and swaying as each starter was being announced. (Akron Beacon Journal, Phil Masturzo)

Later during his freshman year, LeBron began to gain more confidence and started to take over leadership of the team. (Patty Burdon)

LeBron celebrates his first high school state championship with senior leader Maverick Carter (in the middle raising the trophy) and sharp-shooting junior guard Chad Mraz (with a towel over his head). (Akron Beacon Journal, Phil Masturzo)

Even when LeBron was just a sophomore, members of the media couldn't wait to stick cameras and microphones in his face. LeBron handled himself like a veteran. (Patty Burdon)

Gloria was usually very animated while she attended LeBron's games, wearing a game jersey with "LeBron's Mom" embroidered on the back. (Akron Beacon Journal, Phil Masturzo)

One of the biggest disappointments in LeBron's athletic career came his sophomore year, when St. Vincent-St. Mary lost to Oak Hill Academy by a single point. LeBron took the loss hard. (Akron Beacon Journal, Phil Masturzo)

LeBron was becoming big news, at least in Akron, by his sophomore year. Here, he poses for the *Akron Beacon Journal* in front of St. Vincent Church, across the street from the high school. (Akron Beacon Journal, Phil Masturzo)

Despite outside media attention, LeBron was like any other kid in school. Here, on Spirit Day, he goofs around with friends. (Akron Beacon Journal, Phil Masturzo)

LeBron was usually all smiles on the basketball court—perhaps because he felt more at home there than anywhere else. (Akron Beacon Journal, Phil Masturzo)

LeBron and Gloria shared an unusually strong bond—as much best
friends as mother and son.
(Akron Beacon Journal, Phil Masturzo)

LeBron with coach Dru Joyce II while in Chicago for a postseason All-Star game. Joyce coached
LeBron in AAU and high school and was also a close family friend. (Akron Beacon Journal, Phil Masturzo)

LeBron showed an unusual intensity for a high school player. Here, he looks for an opening in order to make a play. (Akron Beacon Journal, Phil Masturzo)

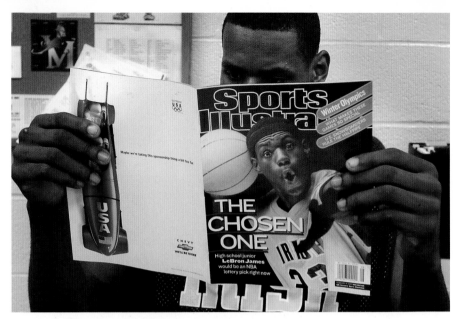

LeBron reading about LeBron. *Sports Illustrated* featured LeBron on its cover during his junior year. It was only the eighth time the national weekly had so featured a high school ballplayer in its 47-year history. (Akron Beacon Journal, Phil Masturzo)

LeBron, a junior, shakes hands with Carmelo Anthony, a senior. LeBron would become the No. 1 pick in the 2003 NBA draft; Anthony, the No. 3 pick in that draft. They also became friends. (Akron Beacon Journal, Phil Masturzo)

LeBron drives to the basket for 2 of his 36 points against Oak Hill Academy, the perennial national power that was No. 1 in the country at the time in 2002. Carmelo Anthony finished with 34 points, but "Melo" got the last laugh as Oak Hill prevailed 72-66.
(Akron Beacon Journal, Phil Masturzo)

LeBron put on a show in the state championship game his junior year against Cincinnati's St. Bernard Roger Bacon high school, but despite his dunks and other crowd-pleasing moves, the Irish lost.
(Patty Burdon)

incoming freshmen, focusing on the older players. They liked the way Maverick had handled himself over the years and decided to give the honor to the senior. When Rogers told Dambrot of the choice, he was surprised by the coach's reaction.

"I told Tim, 'That's great, except, he's not even the best player on our team,'" said Dambrot. "I told him LeBron was our best player. Then I told him LeBron was the best player in the state."

(Maverick was good enough to go on to play college ball at Western Michigan University, though he transferred to Akron after one year to become a business major.)

While reporters recognized LeBron's skills and were impressed to see such quality basketball being played by someone so young, they thought Dambrot was off base. Maverick Carter was the team's top scorer. LeBron had averaged just eight points a game. This kid was only a freshman; he still had plenty of flaws in his game. And when Dambrot mentioned he thought LeBron could go straight into the NBA from high school, they thought he was downright crazy.

But the reporters saw only the present. Dambrot was looking at the future.

NINE

EDDIE

Gloria and Eddie Jackson were a regular presence at LeBron's games. Gloria would typically arrive fashionably late to games, and she had it down to a science. After hugging and kissing all of her family and friends in the stands, working the crowd like a politician, she would make her way to her seat just before the opening tip.

Eddie needed to be in his seat as soon as the team stepped out onto the court for warmups. And he had his reason.

Eddie had been a star track athlete at Buchtel High School in Akron, a local athletic powerhouse school in virtually every sport. "A lot of people didn't have their mother or father in the stands," he said, "but my father was always there at my sporting events. Before every race, I wanted my father to be the last person I saw before I came out of the starting blocks."

Jackson remembers the disappointment he felt when, at one meet, he got himself situated in the starting blocks and looked up to see the reassuring face of his father, only to realize that his father wasn't in the crowd. Jackson knew there had to be a reason why his dad wasn't there, but it didn't matter. All he knew was that the familiar face that calmed him down before each race wasn't there.

"This particular race was the regionals and I had a chance

to make it to state," said Jackson. "I got in the starting blocks and I didn't see my father. I hit every single hurdle on the track. I think I came in seventh or dead last."

Each time Eddie attended one of LeBron's games, he would always show a sign, whether it was a wave, some sort of noise to get LeBron's attention, or just a little nod. He always wanted to make sure that he would be there when LeBron looked up.

Eddie was lucky to be free to attend LeBron's games.

Eddie Jackson came to understand that there were no guarantees in life. He had been emotionally lost when he moved into the James's home, and after Freda's death he seemed to reel in ways that were to affect everyone. That was why he was in the newspapers long before LeBron. On March 21, 1991, he was the subject of a Metro Section story in the *Akron Beacon Journal* headlined, "Akron Man Charged In Schoolyard Cocaine Sale." The article stated, in part: "A 24-year-old Akron man could face up to 25 years in prison because he allegedly sold drugs on school property.

"Eddie G. Jackson, Jr. of Hardesty Boulevard was arrested shortly after 5 p.m. Tuesday on a charge of aggravated drug trafficking.

"Detectives said Jackson sold to an undercover officer a half-ounce of cocaine for $700 while in the parking lot at Roswell Kent Middle School, 1445 Hammel St."

The offense was a minor felony because Jackson sold to an undercover officer and there was no indication that he ever sold to a child. But because the sale was within 1,000 feet of a schoolyard, an extra two years were tacked on the prison sentence.

Eddie should have known how disappointing the incarceration of a parent would be to a child; his own mother, Madeline Garrett, had been convicted of aggravated murder and sentenced to two concurrent life terms in the Ohio Reformatory for Women in Marysville three years earlier. Eddie was the oldest of her four sons; the youngest was only 14 when he had to visit his mother in prison.

Eddie was lucky to be released after 27 months.

When media interest in LeBron began to grow during high school, the question began to be raised about LeBron's real father.

LeBron wouldn't discuss the topic, because to him, it was a nonissue. The man he calls dad is Eddie Jackson. But fame has a way of pressing an issue, and the topic kept coming up.

It was reported in an article in *ESPN The Magazine* in December of 2002 that LeBron's father was a "casual sex partner named Anthony McClelland" who had spent time in jail for arson and theft. McClelland seems to have made the claim. Frankie Walker, Sr. remembered McClelland coming to him after being released from jail. Walker said McClelland thanked him for being a role model and mentor for his son, LeBron, during his younger years.

McClelland frequently called the *Akron Beacon Journal*, leaving messages to say that he was in fact LeBron's father. McClelland claimed to have trophies and awards at his house that belonged to LeBron. "I don't know what Anky is trying to prove," Bruce Kelker said, using McClelland's nickname. "He ain't the father."

Another name that surfaced as the possible biological father was Roland Bivins. He was a charming young man, athletic, charismatic, and oh, how the ladies took a liking to him, Gloria James included. Roland was a basketball player, and his six-foot frame seemed to glide across the basketball court while he played at Central-Hower High School in Akron.

"I have no proof and I'm not trying to make any judgments

or anything like that, but to me, it makes a great deal of sense if the father is Roland," said a former assistant coach at Central-Hower who coached Bivins. "He was a lady-killer, a handsome young man, and his smile was a mile long, just like LeBron's. Roland was an exceptional athlete with great leaping ability."

Bruce Kelker, who was a friend of Bivins's, also noticed similarities. "He had that personality where if you knew him, you loved him, and LeBron is the same way."

The question was left unanswered, though, when Bivins was murdered in a dispute in 1994. The police report stated that Roland had two sons at the time of his death, Roland, 11, and Derrick 5. Roland's obituary did not mention LeBron, who was nine at the time.

To LeBron, though, the answer—indeed the question—was irrelevant: Eddie Jackson was the only father he ever knew. Whenever LeBron accepted any type of award, he would thank his mother, Gloria, his father, Eddie Jackson, and his teammates and coaches. Jackson made it a habit of attending not only games, but practices as well. He may have dressed like he came right off the set of a Jay-Z video, he may have been cool, he may have looked very young for his age, yet he didn't act like he was just one of LeBron's boys. He was still "dad."

As always, Gloria and LeBron seemed unaffected by the public speculation. As long as they had each other, to hell with what anyone else was thinking.

TEN

SOPHOMORE YEAR

In their sophomore year, LeBron, Dru, Willie, and Sian were already the heart of one very talented team when Romeo Travis joined them at St. Vincent-St. Mary. The four best friends were about to become the "The Fab Five."

At first, though, Romeo didn't seem to fit in.

Romeo was a transfer student from Central-Hower, one of eight public high schools in Akron. His mother switched schools to keep him out of trouble, but when Romeo transferred to St. Vincent-St. Mary, he entered a completely different environment from the one he was used to.

"I hated it at Saint V and I wanted to go back home," Romeo said.

The other players, who had become like brothers—without the sibling rivalry—weren't thrilled about the newcomer, either. LeBron had known Romeo in eighth grade at Riedinger, but the other three immediately clashed.

"I didn't like Romeo at all," Sian said later. "We almost fought. He was selfish when he got here. He didn't know how to share, and that was important to all of us, because we had been together on and off the court for so long, and we were like family. We shared everything, and that's what families are supposed to do. I'm not talking about greedy and always wanting stuff like food. I'm talking about sharing your friendship, and your feelings, and sharing, you know, love for a 'brotha.'"

"I didn't like Sian. I hated Dru, and Willie didn't like me over a girl," Romeo said. "I hated sharing. I hated to give up anything. It got to the point where I was so selfish that I would eat my food, and if I was full, I wouldn't ask anybody if they wanted some. I'd just throw it away. I went to a public school, and while I was there I just learned that you had to get what you could get," said Romeo.

That philosophy didn't fly with Sian and his friends, because they had come to realize that the way to be successful on the court and in life was to share and trust the people who were most important to you.

"So what we did as a group is we started to be selfish toward Romeo," Sian said. He had to realize that if he was going to be here with us and share in what we were trying to do as a basketball team, he was going to have to change. He was still set in his ways. He hated sharing, but we always needed to share with each other because we were around each other so much. He'd ask for something and you would give it to him, because that's how we were, but then when you'd ask him for something, he'd be like, 'No.'"

Romeo, a candy "junkie" whose pockets bulged with Skittles, M&M's, Lemonheads, and others, said that one day "I was eating some Skittles in the red bag. When I was eating those Skittles, I saw that somebody had bought doughnuts, and I needed some of those doughnuts. Somebody asked me for some Skittles and I gave them some."

It seemed like a very insignificant gesture, but Romeo, for the first time finally sharing something of his with the rest of his friends—it was monumental. Giving up even one piece of candy was, for Romeo, a major sacrifice. He showed them that he finally understood their attitude that you had to give in order to receive. That day, the four friends became five.

There was already talk about a repeat of the state championship. And why not? These kids, who had already played so well together, for so long, were only going to get better. And they did.

During LeBron's sophomore year, the Irish charged through the season, finishing the year with a 27-1 record.

The one loss stands out, though even in comparison with the previous year's undefeated season, it hardly detracts from the success of the Fab Five's sophomore year. In fact, that one loss put the kids from St. Vincent-St. Mary in the national spotlight for the first time.

The game was against Virginia's vaunted Oak Hill Academy, the perennially top-ranked national basketball school, played in the National Hoops Classic at Battelle Hall in downtown Columbus.

LeBron considered it the biggest game of the year for his team; it would give them a chance to see how they stacked up against the country's best basketball players.

That year, Oak Hill had DeSagana Diop, a seven-foot center (who would be selected eighth overall, in the 2001 NBA draft). Six Oak Hill players would go on to play Division I college ball.

The St. Vincent-St. Mary teammates knew they were underdogs—something they weren't used to being. Their coaches thought they had a real chance to knock off the powerhouse. Assistant coach Steve Culp scouted Oak Hill three or four times before the matchup, and he and Dambrot both felt Oak Hill wasn't very sound defensively.

They might have been alone in that opinion.

"I was telling people we were going to win the game, and they looked at me like I was crazy," Culp said. "We just had to convince the kids."

"We weren't worried about LeBron. We knew he would be ready," Culp said. "Once the rest of the kids bought into what we told them, we felt good."

Maybe until they stepped out onto the court.

"Seriously, to keep it real, I didn't know what to think," LeBron said. "I'm looking at our team, and I love my guys, but then I see Oak Hill walk in and I was like, 'WOW.' I thought we had no chance."

St. Vincent-St. Mary played an exceptional game, and LeBron, as he became accustomed to doing, stepped up and delivered, hitting some shots that were almost unbelievable, considering that here was a sophomore playing against the top high school players in the U.S. LeBron seemed able just to float the ball over Diop inside. As with most high school teams, the Irish didn't get to practice much against seven-footers. But LeBron made adjustments on the spot, with two and sometimes three defenders guarding him.

To the Columbus fans, St. Vincent-St. Mary were Ohio's David to Oak Hill's Goliath, and they cheered on the kids from Akron.

The Irish led 52-42 in the early minutes of the third quarter, but the Oak Hill Warriors fought back. St. Vincent-St. Mary held a seven-point lead with a little more than three minutes left in the game when LeBron's legs started to cramp up. The intense action was starting to take its toll. He sat for just a short time—maybe less than a minute—then reentered the game.

He wasn't the same, though. The short rest had thrown his rhythm off; his shot was flat, because he didn't have enough leg strength to get off the ground. With the game in the balance in the final minute, LeBron missed a 13-foot jumper and two free throws, and his final jumper from just inside the three-point line, right at the buzzer, rolled in and out.

It was a valiant effort by LeBron, a skinny, 6-foot-6, 16-year-old who was named the game MVP with a game-high 33 points. But as Oak Hill celebrated its close win, LeBron sobbed uncontrollably on the court. He had wanted nothing more than to carry his team on his back.

"I know to this day, LeBron never got over that loss," Culp said later. "There are certain games that you will always keep with you as an athlete, games that you just don't forgot. There is no doubt that the Oak Hill game his sophomore year hurt more than any other."

For St. Vincent-St. Mary, the loss marked the end of a 36-game win streak. It also marked a turning point in St. Vincent-St. Mary's basketball program. The team had learned a great deal about itself. These players were now confident that they were at the same level as the best. They had arrived.

Still, it was a painful way to arrive, a heart-piercing defeat for a group of young kids from Akron who had felt invincible.

"It's supposed to hurt," Dambrot said after the game, his eyes blood-shot red. The coaches, too, were in tears, because they felt so bad for the kids. Everything had seemed scripted just right for the Irish to pull the upset. "We executed our game plan to near perfection," Dambrot said.

LeBron later composed himself enough to face the media, and he put the loss in perspective.

"I'm proud of everybody, the players, the coaches, the fans, everybody," he said. "We had a chance to win, but the shot just wouldn't go in."

As LeBron spoke to the press, you could tell he was replaying that last-second shot over and over. "It hurts, but we got all the tears and the frustration and disappointment out of our system and it's time to get back to work."

Keith Dambrot had taken LeBron and his friends through a quantum leap in skills. But he yearned to return to college athletics, and he decided to move on when he got the opportunity at the end of the season.

Dambrot's stay at St. Vincent-St. Mary wasn't very long, only three years. Had he stayed two more years, he might well have won four state titles. As it was, he compiled a 69-10 record and won two consecutive Division III state championships. But he felt it was time to move on. He returned to the college ranks as an assistant at the University of Akron, in the Mid-American Conference—the same conference he had been forced out of as a head coach.

For Dambrot, returning to coach in college was the culmination of an eight-year struggle, but leaving the high school, and one of the best players in the country, was difficult. He knew that his decision to leave hurt the kids.

"They didn't like it at first," Dambrot recalled. "I could tell they were mad at me, because for about three weeks LeBron wouldn't call me coach. He just called me Mr. Dambrot."

But LeBron realized what the opportunity meant to his coach. "I was very happy for him," LeBron said. "He waited a very long time to get back into college coaching."

Dambrot could only look back with wonder when he thought about it.

"You don't think I'll be forever grateful? I got fired at Central Michigan, never thought I'd ever coach again at any level, then I get the best player in the country. I said to myself, how does that happen? Think about that. After being accused of being a racist I get to coach LeBron James, who some say was one of the best high school basketball players ever. The irony is just unbelievable."

ELEVEN

FIVE-STAR

Basketball camps are an unusual phenomenon. The biggest ones are gathering grounds for talented kids from around the country to compete with each other, to pick up some of the finer points of the game, and—sometimes more importantly—to show off their stuff. The camps are popular haunts of college scouts, who may decide who gets a scholarship offer based on what they see there. They're also an important testing ground for representatives of athletic equipment companies, who are there shilling their product—and watching for the future stars who might become their pitchmen.

LeBron was invited to one of the premier summer basketball camps—the Five-Star Basketball Camp at Robert Morris University's Sewall Center in Pittsburgh. He would not be the first exceptional athlete to attend the camp. Moses Malone also attended, and later became the first high school player to be drafted directly into the NBA. Not all examples would necessarily inspire, though. Lenny Cooke was a previous high school phenomenon who attended the camp; he declared that he would join the NBA after graduation, essentially throwing a party for himself to which no one came—he was not drafted.

The Five Star Camp, though, was *the* place to play if you

were hoping to get a college scholarship. NBA-potential talent was sometimes seen; likely Division-I recruits were a given.

By applying what he learned at the Five-Star camp, a student with adequate grades and minimally good college entrance exam scores could get the extra boost needed for a full-ride college scholarship. LeBron, as far as anyone could tell, might be one of the lucky inner-city kids to play his way to a college his mother otherwise couldn't afford.

The longtime and legendary Five-Star Basketball Camp director Howie Garfinkel saw the hype machine coming when LeBron was a junior and playing in his prestigious camp. Garfinkel, a native of Manhattan, had received a call from St. Vincent-St. Mary assistant coach Steve Culp, who regularly worked the camp in Pittsburgh, telling Garfinkel he *had* to take this young kid.

"We were looking forward to seeing a very fine young prospect," Garfinkel said. "Out of this league, there's been something like 125 players [who have gone] into the NBA. So LeBron comes, he's on a team, and the first game I saw him I think it was the second or third game of the day and he's totally dominant. He's dominating the league, killing everyone. He's 6'-5" and a great passer, he had range on his jump shot. It was obvious we were watching a star of the future."

Around the fourth game, midway through the week, Garfinkel decide that LeBron was just too good for the underclassmen's league he was in, which Garfinkel called the development league. Future stars who had played in the development league included Billy Owen, Christian Laettener, Grant Hill, Malik Sealy, Bobbie Hurley, Ron Artest, Corey Magette, and Dajuan Wagner, to name a few.

"We don't like to move kids out of the development league, but he was just so good, we had to give him a shot," Garfinkel said.

The league for seniors was called the NBA. When one player already in the "NBA" became injured, Garfinkel decided to move LeBron to his place. He went over to LeBron to tell him that he was being promoted. But LeBron he didn't want to leave his team. "So we let him play in both," Garfinkel said.

Garfinkel said he worked out the schedule so that the two teams would not have to play games at the same time. From that point on to the end of the camp, LeBron played in both leagues, and instead of playing two games a day, he played four.

LeBron was so outstanding in both leagues that he played in both All-Star games. "No one has ever played in both before LeBron, no one has done it since, and I doubt if anyone will ever do it again."

Garfinkel also noted how LeBron handled the media.

"He was so down to earth. He handled celebrity beautifully in my opinion. I saw a lot of seniors come out of these games with attitudes and it went to their heads. LeBron was never like that. He loves the game, he works hard at the game, and as far as the media, the media is doing their job. The media does their job, he's getting the publicity, and it's well-deserved."

Garfinkel compared LeBron with other great high school players. "He's definitely in the mix with the best high school players of all times. I'm not going to say he's the best, because I saw Calvin Murphy score 34 points in an All-Star game one night, then have to travel to Allentown, where he scored 62 points in 29 minutes the next night in a major All-Star game. On the next level, you have Wilt Chamberlain and Connie Hawkins. LeBron is the best passer for his size since Magic Johnson. And I'm going to put him with Bird and Johnson and as far as the best passing big men I've ever seen. Those three—Magic, Bird, and LeBron."

LeBron had the natural ability to play basketball better

than almost anyone his age. But that had nothing to do with moving into the world of professional athletics without losing your soul. As Garfinkel knew well, there were a lot of things heading toward LeBron that the young man couldn't possibly be prepared for. How would he handle himself if his picture started appearing on magazine covers, if his favorite sports-casters started begging him for interviews, if adults started seeking his autographs? How would he deal with strange new pressures?

"It's ruined a lot of kids who couldn't handle it," said Garfinkel. "If he's got a strong support system who tells him he's not the greatest, he'll be okay. If he starts to believe his press clippings. . . ."

TWELVE

FOOTBALL

LeBron was already being compared to Kobe Bryant, the L.A. Lakers' All-Star who a few years earlier had gone directly to the NBA from high school. (In fact, both Bryant and LeBron expressed annoyance at how frequently they were compared in the media.) He was clearly a *basketball* phenom, and that's how most outsiders thought of him.

Some observers, though, were more interested in LeBron as a *football* player. They thought he had the makings of a young Randy Moss, the All-Pro receiver for the Minnesota Vikings.

That comparison might sound a little far-fetched, but three men with solid NFL credentials who coached LeBron on the gridiron said he had the talent.

Jay Brophy, head football coach at St. Vincent-St. Mary, said he had no doubt that LeBron could have played in the NFL. Brophy was a linebacker and the captain of the Miami Hurricanes team that defeated Nebraska in the Orange Bowl and won the 1983 National Championship; in his first season with the Miami Dolphins, he started in five games, played in Super Bowl XIX, and was voted the Dolphins' Rookie of the Year.

Mark Murphy, an assistant coach on Brophy's staff, seconded the opinion. Murphy played 12 seasons in the NFL, all with the Green Bay Packers as a strong safety. He was enshrined in the Packers' Hall of Fame in 1998 after totaling 900 tackles, 20 interceptions, and 11 quarterback sacks. Also in agreement was St. Vincent-St. Mary alum Frank Stams, Jr., an All-American linebacker at Notre Dame, who was named the Defensive MVP of the 1989 Fiesta Bowl, when the Irish won the national championship; he played for the Los Angeles Rams, the Kansas City Chiefs, and fulfilled his childhood dream of playing for the Cleveland Browns.

LeBron was an all-state performer as a wide receiver during his sophomore and junior seasons. Because he was so tall and much bigger than the average high school receiver, he made the game look easy. When he lined up as a wide receiver, he just had the look of a Division I college player on the verge of stardom. He didn't look gangly or awkward in his uniform, as do many tall basketball players when they get on the football field.

As a 14-year-old freshman, LeBron started out on the freshman team but made some big catches—enough to grab the attention of the coaches. Brophy, then an assistant coach on the varsity squad, remembers hearing about the kid and taking time to watch one of his games with Mark Murphy.

One particular play caught their attention. LeBron, who was a gangly 6'-4" at the time, went over the middle to make a spectacular catch. "It looked like he caught the ball 12 feet in the air," Brophy recalled. "Right then and there, Mark and me knew we had to get him up [to varsity.]"

LeBron was promoted to varsity but didn't make much of an impact, because the ball was seldom thrown to him. His good friend Maverick Carter, a senior, was the go-to receiver.

In the last game of the season, with the Irish trailing in a tight game that would decide a trip to the postseason, LeBron caught nine passes in the fourth quarter, but St. Vincent-St. Mary lost by two points. "If we would've used LeBron more, with the talent we had, we would've won the state championship," Brophy said.

By his sophomore season, LeBron was commanding double- and triple-team coverage and was still making the spectacular catches. He was often able to make a big play in the clutch.

He was tall and deceptively fast. But as with basketball, the trait that LeBron possessed that most impressed his coaches was his knowledge of the game.

"He'd come to the sideline and tell me what coverage the defense was in, and that he would be open in the curl pattern—and sure enough, he was right," Brody said. "He knew how to anticipate what the defense was going to do, and he was good at recognizing tendencies that they had, which allowed us to change plays, even at the line of scrimmage. Those are things that you can never teach, you just have that ability or you don't."

In his sophomore season, LeBron caught 42 passes for 840 yards and 11 touchdowns and was named to the Division IV All-Ohio first team.

Before his junior season, though, he had a decision to make. As a bona fide Division-I college prospect in basketball—even a candidate for the NBA draft—some assumed he would have to give up the more dangerous football and concentrate on "his" sport instead.

LeBron, though, wanted to have fun in high school, and that meant playing the sport that was his first, true love: football.

"When LeBron got back from playing basketball all summer," said Brophy, who had become the head coach, "he couldn't stay away from the football field. I remember one morning, we all had to be here at 9 a.m. I walked in the weight room and there was LeBron. I just cracked up, because the kid loved the game so much, he just couldn't stay away."

Gloria, however, wasn't thrilled with the idea. With a lucrative NBA future on the horizon, Gloria and LeBron were on the verge of financial independence, and one crossing pattern on the football field, one hard hit from a kid just itching at the chance to take out LeBron James, could have ruined that dream of financial freedom. When LeBron decided he was going to play football his junior year, Gloria played it safe and took out an insurance policy to cover LeBron in case he got injured.

"I don't think Gloria was happy with his decision, only because she was worried about him getting hurt," Brophy said. "After she realized LeBron was going to play, she called me and said, "Jay, take care of my baby." Later LeBron said he had decided to play football after the tragic death of young R & B singer Aaliyah, who died in a plane crash a few days earlier. "We're not guaranteed tomorrow," LeBron said. "My mother knows that you have to make the most of your life, because tomorrow you may not even wake up."

Because LeBron made his decision to play at the last minute, he hadn't practiced enough to satisfy Ohio High School Athletic Association rules and so had to miss the first game of the season. LeBron was on the sideline for the season-opening game that Friday night, and even though he wasn't dressed in pads he still felt part of the team. At the end of the game, one of the first people to congratulate coach Brophy was LeBron. "He jumped into my arms like we just won the national championship," Brophy said. "That's how excited he was. He's so passionate about everything that he does."

The following Monday, LeBron was at practice in full pads. Brophy hoped there wouldn't be any dissention or hard feelings, because with LeBron joining the team late someone was going to lose a job. The team welcomed LeBron, though. They were all friends and they weren't going to cast him aside. They knew he was a special player. Tom McDonald, a senior captain at the time, had a meeting with Brophy and they agreed that LeBron should be allowed back on the team. Brophy left the decision up to the team and fully intended to support their decision, regardless of the outcome. But Brophy knew all along that they would vote to have LeBron back.

The following week, when LeBron finally got a chance to play, he was still answering to critics after that game about his decision to play football.

"People can say I'm stupid, but it's my decision to make, and I feel it's the right one," he told reporters. "There is no way I can make people understand what I'm feeling, but the NBA will be there some day. All the fun I'm having in high school won't."

LeBron didn't play defense, so Brophy used him as quarterback on the scout team offense (playing against the first-stringers in practice). "When he was running the scout team offense, he wanted to beat our No. 1 defense. He would throw the ball 60 yards, run the option like a major college quarterback; this kid wanted to win in everything he did." Brophy, LeBron, and the Irish went on to have a successful season that year. St. Vincent-St. Mary went 10-4, won the Region 13 championship, and lost in the Division IV state semifinal game. Even after missing one game, LeBron finished the year with 52 receptions for 1,310 yards and 15 touchdowns, and again was a first-team all-state selection.

The stakes got just too high by his senior year, and LeBron finally decided to give up football.

He had proven that he was one of the best football players in the state, but that wasn't why he played.

"For me, it was just all about going out there and doing

what I loved to do, which was play football," LeBron said. "I just wanted to be out there with my friends and teammates having fun. That was the most important thing for me."

Brophy knew that although LeBron played the game for the fun of it, he played it hard and he played it well because he loved to win—and knew that he could.

"What separates LeBron from other athletes is that his competitiveness rivals no one," Brody said. "If you challenged him in racquetball and you beat him, he'd be a gracious loser; he'd go practice for a week, then call you for a rematch and kick your ass. He had a refuse-to-lose attitude about everything that he did. To me, the biggest thing I saw in LeBron was his ability to handle defeat and learn from it to make him better. Sometimes athletes can't handle defeat, then all of a sudden their confidence is gone. Why do freshmen start in college? Because they believe they can. They believe in their abilities. It's all about self-confidence."

And self-confidence, Brody saw firsthand, was not a problem for LeBron. "I've told LeBron, before you believe the hype, believe in yourself because if you have a bad game, do you think those same guys are going to hype you up? Hell no. Those same guys that pumped you up are the same guys that can't wait to see you fall. Only two people can help you, God and yourself, and LeBron is different in this way: no one can discourage him because he believes in himself."

THIRTEEN

JUNIOR YEAR

When St. Vincent-St. Mary won its second consecutive state title during LeBron's sophomore year, the media attention, at least in the Northeast Ohio area, started to become intense. During LeBron's junior year, it became surreal.

The school year started out peacefully for St. Vincent-St. Mary and LeBron. Home life was stable in Spring Hill. LeBron was doing well in school academically. The basketball team worked together so well and so smoothly as to belie the ages of the players. Although the team's popular coach, Keith Dambrot, had left at the end of the previous season, their new coach was an old friend—Dru Joyce III. Coach Dru had worked with these kids for the previous two years as a volunteer assistant coach and had worked with some of them much longer (including, of course, Little Dru for his whole life.) He had been hired by the school with Dambrot's strong endorsement.

Outside the school, though, there were ever-louder rumblings of interest in the team and in LeBron especially.

The new season schedule for the basketball team included several more nonleague games that would take them on the road to other cities. Coach Dru and many of his players were used to traveling farther for games from their AAU days. These additional games would allow the team to play more often against better caliber opponents. And the more places the team visited, the more people became interested in their star player.

LeBron had received some of his first real national publicity his sophomore year when *SLAM*, a basketball magazine for the Hip-Hop generation, ran a major story on him. The magazine's younger readers wanted to know more about guys their age doing something the rest could only dream about. For LeBron's junior year, the editors had him keep a diary, which was edited and published each month.

But LeBron mania was truly ignited when *Sports Illustrated* came calling.

In America's media-crazed society, certain types of public exposure determine which people will be declared "famous." For politicians, an appearance on CNN or *Meet the Press* probably tops the list. For entertainers, it's Leno or Letterman or *People*. If you're an athlete, it's *Sports Illustrated*.

On February 18, 2002, LeBron James, a 16-year-old inner-city kid playing for a small parochial school in Akron, Ohio, appeared on the cover of *Sports Illustrated* wearing a green "Irish" jersey with No. 23 and a headband without a logo, holding a basketball, his face showing an expression that seemed slightly startled. Beside his photograph were three words: "The Chosen One." Even if LeBron had been silent about his plans regarding college, perhaps even uncertain of it himself, *Sports Illustrated* had spoken loud and clear to the college recruiters: look out, this kid is going straight to the pros.

The article, by sportswriter Grant Wahl, suggested that LeBron would, were he not just a high school junior, be picked—right now—by an NBA team for his abilities. In the article, former NBA player and coach Danny Ainge was quoted as saying, "If I were a general manager, there are only four or five NBA players that I wouldn't trade to get him right now." He went on to mention Jason Williams, then at Duke, and Yao Ming (who would be the No. 1 pick in the 2002 draft) but said, "If LeBron came out this year, I wouldn't even have to think about it. I'd take him No. 1."

Suddenly, the center of the high-school basketball universe shifted. It wasn't New York or L.A. any more. It was moving to blue-collar Rubber City. Akron, Ohio, became the focus of every young high school player in the nation who tuned in to ESPN, watched the sports segments on the news, and read the sports magazines. Some wanted to be like LeBron. Others, maybe, wanted to take him down a notch.

It was a role reversal for the St. Vincent-St. Mary squad: LeBron, Dru, Willie, Sian, Romeo, and the others had been excited to play teams like Oak Hill Academy in order to prove themselves against the best. Now, other schools were taking aim at *them*. On the basketball court, LeBron, already the player against whom opposing teams designed their game plans, now became something of a marked man. Teams could hardly wait for their shot at "The Chosen One."

The first game after the *Sports Illustrated* article came out was against George Junior Republic, a reform school about 45 minutes from Pittsburgh. The game was at Youngstown State University's Beeghley Center, 45 minutes from Akron, and it was a sold-out arena. The game was physical—*very* physical. LeBron, who had scored 36 points in the previous week's game, was the target of the opponent's defense.

Gloria, watching from the stands as usual, got so outraged at one particularly rough foul against LeBron that she ran out onto the court to protest and had to be restrained—by LeBron, who sent her back to the stands. (The incident added to her image as an eccentric and fueled criticism by sportswriters and some fans for her particularly rambunctious behavior in the stands.)

The game continued with the same intensity, the score tied at the end of regulation time. Finally, in overtime, George Junior came out on top, 58-57.

"George Junior, they played well," Coach Joyce said during a press conference after the game. "And as you can imagine, our kids are hurting because this is the first time they've ever had back-to-back losses. No excuses, but our schedule is such that it's starting to take a toll, and the pressure is beginning to wear on them. These are 17-year-olds and I don't care who you are, no team in the country is under the pressure we're under."

Off the court, too, LeBron was beginning to feel the pressure. Everyone suddenly wanted a piece of him. He had become a celebrity. And the school had a problem—there were now security issues they had never anticipated.

The number of journalists coming to the games increased. For the first time in the history of the basketball program, the locker room was off limits to everyone, including the reporters who had been covering the Fab Five since the beginning of their high school play. Before the *Sports Illustrated* article, a sportswriter could walk into the locker room after a game, sit right next to LeBron at his locker, and ask him about the game. Now, press conferences were arranged, with two head coaches and two athletes from each team being brought out to talk, then taken back to the locker room.

Practices were interrupted frequently with adults sneaking into the school to watch practice. Some would send their own children in to try to get the magazines signed.

"I don't like to use foul language, but that pissed me off," LeBron said. "Everybody comes up to me, all these grown folks, asking for autographs talking about it's for their kids, next thing you know, they're selling it on Ebay."

"He's handling it well, but I'm sure it's getting to him," Coach Dru said. However, when LeBron was allowed to speak for himself, he was honest about his feelings. He said he had had enough and wouldn't sign any more *SI*'s.

"He has no life now," said Coach Dru. "He leaves practice yesterday, he walks out the door trying to get home, and a gentleman came up to him with two arm loads of *Sports Illustrateds* for him to sign.

"Fame has its price. If grown men have trouble dealing with it, how do you prepare a kid for this? The reason you can't prepare him is because it's never happened before. We're all breaking new ground."

The rest of the team didn't seem too bothered by the change in atmosphere and the fact that now seemingly everyone in the sports media would be watching them.

It was partly that the team had scheduled more games against tougher competition that they lost a few more games than the previous year. They had lost, again, to Oak Hill Academy and then to George Junior. It was a reminder that they were not perfect, that on any given day, any team can win. But as intense as these young players were, and as much as the boys hated losing, they managed to control their emotions. The Irish regrouped after the losses and continued to play well.

But the team took one final, tough loss to end the season.

In December, St. Vincent-St. Mary had beaten Cincinnati St. Bernard Roger Bacon in a very competitive game. The Irish won by nine points, but the game was much closer. Either side could have won, and fans who attended the game realized that if there was any team in the state who could beat the Irish, it would be Roger Bacon.

When the two met again in the Division II state title game,

it was the hottest ticket in Columbus. Fans outside Ohio State's Value City Arena were scalping tickets for as much as $150.

A day before the state title game, LeBron made a bold statement. "I'm not guaranteeing a win, but I'm guaranteeing that I'm not letting my team lose," he said. The line in the sand was drawn.

The teams battled each other in front of a record crowd of 18,375. Roger Bacon took a 31-30 halftime lead. Late in the game, the Irish trailed 65-63 when the game came down to the last 30 seconds.

LeBron had the ball. He dribbled up court, and everyone in the arena knew what he would do. He was going to take the shot. Suddenly LeBron crossed mid-court and passed the ball to senior guard Chad Mraz, St. Vincent-St. Mary's outstanding outside shooter. Chad took the shot that everyone had expected from LeBron—and missed.

Roger Bacon rebounded, finished off the game on the free throw line, and pulled off one of the biggest upsets of the year.

"I just didn't want to force anything," said LeBron when asked about the game's end. "Chad was open and I got him the ball. He could've put us up by one, but the whole year I've been looking for my teammates, so nothing was going to change."

After the game, several members of the Irish team were crying, including Romeo and Dru. They tried covering their faces so that no one could see their anguish.

LeBron, emotions in check, walked over to the Roger Bacon players, who were hugging each other and celebrating near its bench, and shook the hand of each and every player, coach, and manager. "I respect them a lot," he said. "I respect their game. I respect everybody on their team. Their fans had negative words to say, but I respect them, too, because they came to show support to their team and if you can beat proved themselves a formidable opponent, winningmore respect for you."

LeBron admitted he had one other regret about the loss. "I'm a little bit upset with myself because I guaranteed a victory," he said. "Instead of me dwelling on this game, it's going to make me a lot more hungrier to come back next year. I'll go home, take a couple days off, then I'm back in the gym. I have to keep working hard because if I don't, someone is going to pass me, and I don't want that to happen. I want to stay the No. 1 player in the country. And hopefully next year, our team will be No. 1 in the country."

LeBron stuck with his commitment to working hard that summer. He and his teammates hit the weight room, hard. During LeBron's junior year, he had been taller than most of his opponents but not necessarily stronger. Working the weight room helped him develop his body, and by the fall, at the start of his senior year, he *looked* like an NBA player.

Before then, though, he got an opportunity to play with some NBA players—and get a taste of the controversy that would boil up around him during his senior year in high school.

In May, 2002 he joined a "pickup" game at Gund Arena— home of the Cleveland Cavaliers.

It was a voluntary workout held by seven Cavaliers players, including guards Bryant Stith and Bimbo Coles, forward Jumaine Jones, Chris Mihm, and center DeSagana Diop.

NBA rules, though, prohibit teams from having contact with players not yet eligible for the draft. The violation didn't cause any trouble for LeBron, but it proved costly for the Cavaliers and their coach.

"I don't think there was anything sinister by the Cavaliers, they just weren't paying attention," NBA Deputy Commissioner Russ Granik told the Associated Press at the time. Still, the NBA fined the Cavaliers $150,000 and suspended their head coach, John Lucas, for the first two games of the 2003 season.

"LeBron was not invited," Gloria James told the Associated Press. She said Diop, who was friends with LeBron, told him about the workout and he just showed. "He wasn't aware of any rule. I told him not to worry about it."

Stith was impressed with LeBron in the workout. "I think he could hold his own in the NBA right now," he said.

LeBron continued to play during the summer before his senior year until he broke his left wrist while in a tournament. Luckily for him it wasn't his shooting hand.

"Breaking my wrist probably made me better. It made me work harder and at the time, I was playing pickup games at school with my cast, on and it made me put everything in perspective and not to take things for granted. By me breaking my wrist, it let me sit back and watch other players play and take away little bits and pieces from everybody's game to get better. It made me tougher and more determined. It taught me you can't go out and play timid, because that's when you get hurt. You just have to attack and play aggressive like I've always done. I've been playing aggressive for 15 years and you can't just let up, because you never know if you're going to wake up the next day."

FOURTEEN

TRYING TO STAY NORMAL

LeBron had lived relatively little of what most people might consider "normal" life in his 17 years. Only in the past couple of years had he found even much stability. But now enormous pressures and temptations would swirl about him as the whirlwind of sports celebrity was whipped up by the news media for his senior year in high school.

School itself was one place where life was surprisingly ordinary for LeBron. The teachers and administrators at St. Vincent-St. Mary meant to keep it that way.

In school, LeBron was seen by teachers and students as the same fun-loving kid he had always been. For example, there were practical jokes, like the time when LeBron was carrying an orange away from the lunch room. As he and his friends walked to their next classes, LeBron saw the open door to a classroom where the students had not yet been dismissed at the end of the period. The teacher's back was turned, and LeBron took the orange and rolled it into the room like a hand grenade about to explode. Some of the students, startled by the unfamiliar object, screamed as if it would explode. Others laughed at the outrageousness. Nobody told the teacher exactly how the orange happened to be rolling across the floor, as LeBron raced down the hall and around a corner so as not to get caught.

He was trying to be a kid.

St. Vincent-St. Mary headmaster Dave Rathz understood that LeBron was the biggest challenge to maintaining school normalcy that the staff could ever imagine. Rathz enjoyed much of the attention the school was receiving. He also took pride in the behavior of LeBron and his teammates—as athletes and students alike.

The trouble started with reporters who tried to sneak into the school. Starting with the beginning of LeBron's senior year, Rathz implemented a rule that no media members would be allowed on the school property until after 3 p.m., when school was let out.

"We knew this wasn't going to be a normal year, but we tried to keep it as normal as possible," Rathz said. "We also made it clear to the students and their parents that we wouldn't tolerate anyone coming in asking for autographs from LeBron, and I'm proud to say that we didn't have very many problems with that inside the school. Everyone went about their business as usual."

The public developed a fantasy about St. Vincent-St. Mary. People wondered what happened in the halls and the classrooms during the school day, if LeBron and the others were treated any different from the rest of the student body. One school official said she was contacted by a member of the press who wanted to know if LeBron sat in a separate area when he ate his lunch. The school official jokingly replied, "Yeah, he sits in a glass room all by himself."

There were students who complained about having the burden of being in circumstances others found exciting and different.

"What school do you go to?" an outsider would ask.

"St. Vincent-St. Mary," the student would reply.

"Oh, I bet those basketball players run the school. No wonder you guys win so many games, you recruit all of those players. It's not fair. Can you get me LeBron's autograph?"

Students in other sports were not limited in what they could do, but by comparison they seemed to be considered secondary. "It's not fair," said one student, who played on the girls' basketball team. "We work just as hard as they do and we get no media coverage."

The school remained under control because everyone followed routine as much as possible.

"LeBron followed the same schedule as everyone else," said Patty Burdon, a long-time staffer at the school. "When he walked down the hall, nobody stopped or starred at him. He was just another student like them. The kids would argue with him like they did anyone else. And some of the girls would even tease him."

The teasing, good natured, was about his ears, which seemed to grow before the rest of his body. This created a bit of awkwardness in his appearance until he finally reached his full height of 6'-8" tall.

LeBron, like every other senior with a serious goal unrelated to academics, had mixed feelings about classwork. The closer he came to the NBA draft, the more classwork was an intrusion. He felt the need to develop his skills by spending more time in the gym, something that was not possible. At the same time, the sameness of class was a help. "Eight to three was my comfort zone," he said. "A lot of people say high school was hard, but for me, it was easy. When you have friends and people there with you that you love, it makes it a lot easier."

Though he also said, "Sometimes it got [to be] too much. Sometimes I would wake up and I didn't want to go to school at all because it drained me out a lot."

Still, he kept up good grades. And St. Vincent-St. Mary was

not the type of school that made special "accommodations" for certain athletes. LeBron was a legitimate student.

"He was never at a point where he had a C and had to battle back," said Beth Harmon, English teacher who had LeBron as a freshman, sophomore, and senior. "He never let himself get to that point, at least not for me. He was always the kid who had his work done and if he didn't do it right the first time, he'd do it right the second time. The attitude he had on the basketball court was the same attitude he had in the classroom."

Even though he was most likely not going to college, as soon as he was eligible he took the Ohio ACT test, required for students going directly to college after graduation.

He continued to get along well with his fellow students, despite the obvious opportunities for discord.

"His relationship with his classmates was great," Harmon said. "It was hard during his senior year. I wouldn't say it was easy because here you had one person getting all the attention, but he respected his classmates and they respected him."

Except, maybe, when they passed by "the wall." The Fab Five weren't class cutups, but they did like to "roast"—make fun of themselves and their classmates. Their roasting was like an informal, one-minute version of the celebrity roasts on television—not mean, but definitely spirited. "The Wall" was just that—a wall, in the hall by the school's library where they would all meet between classes—and classmates who didn't want to get roasted knew to avoid it, especially if you happened to be wearing plaid pants or high waters.

"We weren't mean or anything, but people used to be afraid to walk past the wall," LeBron said. There was a worse fate, though: "We had to be good on the wall upstairs—that was like the suburbs," LeBron said. "The wall downstairs was like the 'hood."

LeBron enjoyed participating in regular school activities. There was a disco party for the students when LeBron was a sophomore. Everything that night was to be a reminder of the dance craze of the 1970s that had been important to some of their parents. LeBron saved enough money to go to a thrift store and find the pieces he needed to adopt a look reminiscent of the movie *Saturday Night Fever*. Then he went onto the dance floor, imitating the dance moves, having a wonderful time and not worrying if he looked silly.

The same was true for Pajama Day when all the students wore pajamas to school. This time LeBron was not prepared. He mentioned that he needed pajamas at the last minute. The night before the special day, Gloria, annoyed but dutiful (like most parents of a teenager), made her way to K-Mart where she bought the largest pair of pajamas in stock—3XXX. The trouble was that almost no one is as tall as LeBron, and stores do not routinely stock clothing for youths his size. The pants were long enough because no one cared if they came low enough to cover his ankles. But he couldn't button the top. Gloria sewed on more material so that LeBron could join the rest of the kids in a day of silliness, away from reporters and photographers.

FIFTEEN

SENIOR YEAR: BIG TIME

While daily life at St. Vincent-St. Mary was providing a haven for LeBron, the basketball team's schedule was putting him and his teammates ever more into the limelight. The games themselves wouldn't be a problem; if there was any-place LeBron was more comfortable than in school it was cer-tainly on the basketball court. But the hype, hoopla, and con-troversy that accompanied LeBron's senior year in high school were destined to play out like a three-ring circus.

Coach Dru Joyce had scheduled still more, and more dis-tant, away games so that his talented ballplayers could prove themselves against the best high school competition in the U.S. Now, a team that had once traveled by bus only to state competitions was flying about the nation.

The decision to allow the St.Vincent-St. Mary High to go on a multi-city tour was controversial. The tour schedule involved traveling to Philadelphia, Pittsburgh, Los Angeles, New Jersey, and North Carolina—visiting more than some Division I col-lege programs did.

Ohio High School Athletic Association (OHSAA) commis-sioner Clair Muscaro did not approve. "I felt (LeBron) was ex-ploited through all the travel out of the state and across the country," he said. "It's not what we [OHSAA] are about. It should be about hopping in the yellow school bus and going 30 or 45 miles to play in a gym and then coming home again. It should not be about flying and limousines and promoters making money."

Coach Dru was outraged at Muscaro's public allegations that he and the school were exploiting LeBron. He had watched the core group of boys work for this dream since eighth grade. They came from mixed backgrounds and began with mixed abilities. They had worked intensely hard in pursuit of the dream of a national championship. He noted that other high school sports, such as baseball and softball, go on out-of-state spring trips to play, and this wasn't much different.

"Clair cannot look me in the eye and tell me to my face that I exploited LeBron James or my players," Coach Dru said. "If Clair thinks this is about money, he is fooling himself. This was about a chance for a group of kids to realize a dream that has been years in the making. If I had it to do all over again, I wouldn't change a thing."

That there was money involved with all this was never denied. The school did received money from promoters for playing in out-of-state games. But it received more money by playing at home; the school moved 18 home games to the University of Akron's Rhodes Arena to accommodate the larger crowds.

James Burdon, chairman of St. Vincent-St. Mary's executive board of trustees, said the games were moved to the 5,942-seat college venue to accommodate the demand for tickets, and not as a way of bringing in more money to the school. The money did come, though. According to figures compiled by the University of Akron athletic department, St. Vincent-St. Mary generated $268,735 during LeBron's junior year and $222,116 his senior year. Those revenues did not include appearance fees, some as high as $10,000, for games played out-of-state.

"Those games were not selected by the school with profit in mind," Burdon said. "They were requested by the coaches as a way to play top-caliber competition."

DATELINE: PHILADELPHIA – The St. Vincent-St. Mary team bus pulled in front of the Double Tree Hotel in downtown Philadelphia, and two men who had driven in from Brooklyn, New York, approached the bus door. Each of the men had a copy of the *Sports Illustrated* article with LeBron on the cover. Coach Joyce informed the men that LeBron wasn't signing autographs, and that the team needed to get into the hotel.

As the players walked into the lobby, all the workers knew about LeBron and the team. They came over to talk with the youths. It was the type of reception normally reserved for professional teams such as the Philadelphia 76ers.

DATELINE: LOS ANGELES – The main course at the famous Lawry's Steakhouse in Beverly Hills was a press conference introducing LeBron and the St. Vincent-St. Mary basketball team. The Irish were in Tinsel Town for a game against No. 4–ranked Mater Dei of Santa Ana at Pauley Pavilion, on the campus of UCLA. To their amazement and delight, the Irish were the No. 1–ranked team.

The trip to L.A. was almost surreal. Here you had high school players stepping out of limousines at a fancy hotel and walking in as if they had won NCAA or NBA titles, with fans clamoring about and whispering "that's him, that's him." If LeBron hadn't already had star status elsewhere in the country, he had it in L.A.

The day before the game, organizers of the event held a

press conference at Lawry's steak house, a location known for hosting sports luncheons including media events surrounding the Rose Bowl. When you entered the lobby then walked down a few steps into the dining area, you could see several collegiate flags hanging from the ceiling: Ohio State, Michigan, Cal, USC, Washington, Wisconsin. The flags represented teams that had played in the Rose Bowl. The Irish, along with the other teams participating in the basketball tournament, were in select company.

For LeBron and his friends, along with members of three other teams, there was lunch of prime rib and potatoes followed by interviews. Each team answered questions in turn, St. Vincent-St. Mary going last.

Coach Joyce and his five senior players—LeBron, Little Dru, Romeo, Sian, and Willie—walked confidently to the table. They were comfortable with the press in ways most kids their age were not. When one reporter asked about the handling of pressure, LeBron said, "It's easy. We're just having fun. We don't look for the publicity. All we want to do is have fun and play basketball together."

LeBron said he had been to Los Angeles before and seen the sights; what made him happy was that his teammates were getting a chance to experience the city. "This may be the only time any of these guys have a chance to come to L.A."

At Pauley Pavilion, fans eagerly awaited what seemed as thought it was the LeBron James Show. The game was again televised by ESPN2 with the same announcers as the first televised game in Cleveland. And this was a game that sportscaster Bill Walton, who had won so many NCAA championships with UCLA in the 1970s on that very court, wasn't going to miss. Walton, who was in Dallas for an NBA game earlier in the day, hopped on a plane and arrived at Pauley Pavilion just in time to do the pregame.

The moment Bill Walton entered Pauley Pavilion, he was in his element. The fans in the first few rows spotted him and began yelling his name. They were not seeing the guy from ESPN; they were still cheering still in response to his brilliant playing days.

For LeBron and the Irish, the crowd was not so generous. They seemed to want either perfection or complete failure. LeBron was warming up, went in for a dunk, and lost the ball into the stands. The crowd booed.

"You know the fans are against you when they boo you during warm-ups," LeBron joked later.

St. Vincent-St. Mary defeated Mater Dei 64-58, LeBron getting 21 points. But it was one of those unsatisfactory victories where even the least sophisticated fan knows that neither team played especially well. "I thought I was going to see this kid take over," one fan said of LeBron. "He didn't show me anything."

During the postgame interviews, reporters from the west coast didn't want to know how the players felt about the game as much as they wanted to know how the travel affected the team, how much school they missed, and if their classwork suffered as a result of all the travel. LeBron answered some of the questions, but Coach Dru began to get upset, especially after a reporter from the *Los Angeles Times* started asking questions about LeBron's grade point average and how schoolwork gets done with so much traveling. They were valid questions, especially when you consider that this was the first time St. Vincent-St. Mary had ever played in L.A. and that the writers from L.A. knew very little about the school. But Coach Dru, who sometimes felt as though the entire press corps was out to get his team or LeBron, became so upset that he stopped the press conference. The next day, the *Los Angeles Times* wrote a scathing piece about the arrogance of LeBron, Coach Dru, the team, and the school.

DATELINE: PITTSBURGH – St. Vincent-St. Mary was scheduled to face New Castle (Pa.) at Mellon Arena at 1 p.m.— the same time the Pittsburgh Steelers were playing. The game didn't start until 5 p.m. Rumor had it that several Steelers stars wanted to watch the game and requested that it be delayed so that they could finish their game, shower, and get to Mellon Arena.

Officials denied the rumor, yet there on hand to watch from the stands were running back Jerome Bettis and wide receivers Plaxico Burress and Hines Ward.

It was to prove a good day for everyone, Pittsburgh defeating Carolina 30-14, and the Irish beating New Castle 82-46, LeBron scoring 32 points.

Midway through the third quarter, during a stop in the action, LeBron caught Bettis's attention. "Y'all win?" LeBron asked the Steeler star.

DATELINE: GREENSBORO, NC – St. Vincent-St. Mary was facing R.J. Reynolds of Winston-Salem, a team that was ranked nationally in the top 10. The Irish still had the No. 1 ranking, but fans inside the Greensboro Coliseum were certain an upset was in the making. Several minutes before the game, a DJ from a local hip-hop radio station, who was entertaining the crowd with music on a turntable, shouted into the microphone: "C'mon fans, get off your rear and let's send LeBron James and St. Vincent-St. Mary home with a loss." The record North Carolina high school crowd of more than 15,000 went crazy.

That got LeBron and his teammates mad. From the opening tip, the Irish dominated, and what North Carolina fans thought would be an upset turned into an all-out rout. LeBron scored 32 points in the Irish 85-56 win.

"Sometimes you have to watch what you wish for," Coach Joyce said later.

DATELINE: TRENTON, NJ – Playing Los Angeles West Chester in the Primetime Shootout tournament at Sovereign Bank Arena, the Irish won in another rout, 78-52, as LeBron scored 52 points. But the trip to New Jersey was to prove an off-the-court learning experience for the St. Vincent-St. Mary players. The players went to Trenton a day before the game and hooked up with a 1977 graduate of St. Vincent-St. Mary, Marty Johnson, also a Princeton graduate and well-respected businessman. He was a social entrepreneur who had earned international recognition for his work in revitalizing Trenton and other urban areas. His organization, Isles of Redevelopment, was started after Johnson worked in Brazil during his junior year at Princeton. The Isles' programs included Youth-Build, which teaches high school dropouts construction skills while they earn a degree.

"We wanted this to be as much of an educational field trip as a basketball tournament," Johnson said. "There's life outside sports.

The games may have seemed more important because of the venues—James A. Rhodes Arena at home, other big-time arenas in big cities on the road, but when LeBron and his team took the court, they were having fun.

Sometimes fans wanted more from the game than even the team members did. "In some instances, the fans were there to be entertained," coach Dru said. "Often times, it wasn't like a group of high school kids cheering their team on. Don't get me wrong, our student body was great, but there were people there waiting to be entertained."

"I didn't play for the crowd," LeBron said. "I played for myself and the team. I just wanted to make sure the crowd was into it. When the crowd came to see us, I didn't like the crowd to be dead. I wanted our crowd to be like Arco Arena [home to the Sacramento Kings] or the Staples Center [Los Angeles Clippers and Lakers], and I just tried make sure they were still awake.

"Every night we came out, we know a lot of people came out to see us lose but I love the crowd. I'd rather have 10,000 people come see us lose then 1,000 people come see us win. I loved the adversity because every night we came out, we knew that we were going to get our opponent's best game; I don't care if we were playing Our Lady of the Elms or Mother of the Blind."

The high-profile road games—and especially the Oak Hill game in Cleveland's CSU Convocation Center—brought out more national media who wanted to get in on the story of this highly-touted high school phenomenon.

Immediately after LeBron's performance in the Oak Hill game on ESPN2, the calls started. CNN called the *Akron Beacon Journal*; morning anchor Leon Harris (a native of Akron) wanted to interview a writer about LeBron the following morning.

Then it was the *CBS Early Show*. Then others.

Not all were doing stories yet, though some sent their representatives to visit Akron and the school and watch a game at Rhodes Arena—they just wanted to see what all the hype was about.

"This is a sports phenomenon and I could understand that," St. Vincent-St. Mary athletic director Grant Innocenzi said. "But when *60 Minutes* called, that's an international news show with some of the most famous and important people in the world. And they wanted to do a story on LeBron and Gloria? That's when I thought to my self, *what did I get myself into here?* ESPN I could handle, but 6*0 Minutes?*"

The *60 Minutes* piece never panned out, but media interest continued to grow throughout the season.

LeBron didn't seem to be worried that the media was making too much out of him. Asked if he was being over hyped, he said, "I don't know. You tell me. I'm just going out there playing my game. Y'all are making all the remarks."

Yet a casual glance at LeBron showed one affect of the media rush: LeBron went nowhere without a belt that looked a little like the one worn by police, though instead of handcuff case and flashlight, his held two separate cellular telephones and a two-way pager. Probably no one would have been surprised had LeBron started moving about with his own satellite uplink.

In October of 2002, the David Letterman show came calling. LeBron wasn't a singer, a dancer, a musician, an actor, a comic, or an author, all staples of late-night television. He was a high school kid who could run up and down a basketball court making baskets, assisting his team, and doing it better than other kids his age. But a variety show like Letterman?

"I remember it was the end of the school day, the phone rang, and we just let the answering machine pick up," said Patty Burdon, public relations director at the school. "When we heard the producer introduce herself and say David Letterman wanted LeBron to be on his late night show, we jumped up and burst out laughing. We must have looked like a couple of kids who'd seen their first celebrity. That was the beginning; we knew we'd just entered another world. And I remember seeing Eddie Jackson that night at practice and I told him about it. He just laughed and asked why they would want

LeBron." Burdon said the show called again in early December and once again a few months later. Jay Leno's producer would call for the same reason later in the season.

Good Morning America called in December, as did the *Live with Regis & Kelly* show (they wanted LeBron to appear on the show and have him shoot some hoops with Regis).

A woman representing the *New Yorker* magazine called to say that a very famous photographer who had photographed Kareem Abdul-Jabbar when he was a young player wanted to photograph LeBron when he was in Trenton.

An independent producer from L.A. called with an idea for a TV show for LeBron.

Actor Martin Lawrence's production company called wanting to hear from LeBron regarding starring in a movie about a young basketball player who goes into the NBA directly from high school. Universal Studios would be doing the movie. Even LeBron laughed about this one.

In a sort of feedback loop, the media's fervor in promoting the next big thing sparked even more interest in LeBron.

St. Vincent-St. Mary athletic director Grant Innocenzi got more unusual requests daily. Several prominent athletes called to speak with LeBron, presumably in order to offer advice.

"I knew this job wasn't going to be normal and I could tell that right from the beginning, with some of the phone calls I got from guys like Emmit Smith, who called more than once," Innocenzi said. "Reggie Jackson wanted to consult with LeBron but didn't want to be known. He wanted to keep it low-key."

Those kinds of calls became common for Innocenzi, not to mention the stacks and stacks of letters he received from people all over the world, asking for some sort of autograph from LeBron. Innocenzi remembers one particular package he received in his office. It was from Spain.

"This kid was 16 and wrote a letter saying how much he loved LeBron. He sent a T-shirt with 'Valencia, Spain' on the front and wanted it signed by LeBron."

Innocenzi forwarded the mail and the requests to LeBron, who obliged the 16-year-old by signing the shirt and sending it back to him. LeBron didn't do that for everyone who wrote a letter or sent him a T-shirt, but in this case he wanted to give something back to a fan thousands of miles away. "I'll do anything for the kids," LeBron said. "I love kids."

Innocenzi said the year he had was something he'll never, ever forget. "It was a once-in-a-lifetime thing. If this ever happens around here again, I'll probably be old, sitting in an easy chair drinking a Martini. It was a great time. It was 80 hours a week from November to March, but it was worth every minute."

One of the wackier requests came from a woman in Akron who was sincere in wanting LeBron to be a guest in her home. According to Innocenzi, a dear old lady called his office and wanted to do something really nice for her husband's birthday. She asked if Innocenzi could ask LeBron come over to the couple's house in Akron for the birthday party. The lady said her husband had lost a step or two but still loved to play basketball. The couple had a basketball hoop in the driveway, from when their kids lived with them, and she suggested that LeBron and her husband could play a little one-on-one until she was done baking the cake, then they could come inside and eat the cake after the game was over. That was one of the requests LeBron *didn't* grant.

SIXTEEN

A ROLE MODEL

You can't choose whether you are a role model or not," LeBron said in an interview with the *Akron Beacon Journal*. "It's just something that has become part of all this for me. And that is fine."

He might not have asked for the job, but LeBron took it seriously. And for someone who had only recently had real need for a role model himself, he seemed surprisingly comfortable in the position. He had seen firsthand the difference a man like Frankie Walker, Sr. or Bruce Kelker or Dru Joyce could make in a boy's life, so he knew he had the potential to help do good things for younger kids, too.

LeBron had not forgotten Elizabeth Park, where he and Gloria had been taken in by so many neighbors; the place and the people never left his heart. During his senior year, he wanted to do something special for the kids who still lived there. It wasn't as though LeBron had since moved into one of the more affluent communities of Akron; he was still living in subsidized housing at Spring Hill. But Elizabeth Park meant so much to LeBron because he grew up there—really grew up there, learning about life and survival.

Gloria and Eddie (who was free from prison and seemingly going straight) and a family friend, Chris Dennis, who helped run an inner-city help organization called Building Independent Communities Through Education And Empowerment (B.I.C.E.E.), had already gotten together to do some giving back.

"His mother and Eddie were always trying to help out people in the community, as far as donating things to the rec centers, especially at Elizabeth Park," Dennis said. "So LeBron wanted to start doing the same."

Together, the four started contacting businesses and companies in the area, asking for donations of school supplies to be given away before the school year. The donations started coming in—backpacks, notebooks, pens, pencils, everything. LeBron was able to get Adidas and Nike gear to give out to kids. LeBron and Dennis were ready to head down to Elizabeth Park to give out the supplies. LeBron was excited about the event because he couldn't wait to see the kids' faces. He was just like them so he knew what it would mean to them to have a hero come back to his community. They took the things to the Elizabeth Park gym. They were ecstatic, as LeBron shook hands, exchanged high-fives, and gave out the school supplies as well as baseball caps. It was an inspirational sight.

"LeBron really got into it," Dennis said. It made him feel really good. It made him feel proud of where he came from."

LeBron also helped hand out bookmarks to 600 schoolchildren at the Akron Community Service Center and Urban League. Along with a photo, the bookmarks included a quote from LeBron: "My achievements in basketball have made me famous, but if I didn't do the work in the classroom, you would never know who I am."

LeBron loved anything that had to do with being a part of a family, mainly because during his childhood he didn't have much of a traditional family upbringing. That's why he was honored to speak at the annual end-of-the-season banquet of his old Pee Wee football team, the South Rangers, during the fall of his senior year in high school. Frankie Walker, Sr., who helped organize the banquet, thought it would be the perfect time to honor some of the South Rangers' players who had had illustrious careers. Walker decided that for this banquet, they would frame three jerseys and hang them at the concession stand at the football field. The three players were LeBron, running back Antonio Pittman, who was an Ohio State recruit, and running back Tyrell Sutton, who was just a freshman in high school at the time. Walker asked LeBron months in advance if he would speak at the banquet. Before Walker could finish asking his request, LeBron agreed.

As the young players, nicely dressed in dress pants and ties, gathered and sat at their tables, everyone was excited about having LeBron speak, even the parents. The mere fact that LeBron returned to his roots made the current South Rangers players and parents proud. "This is a beautiful thing," one father of a player said. "That young man [LeBron] has been pulled in every direction and he took the time to come and speak to these kids. This is something they'll always remember, and as a parent, I really appreciate him coming."

After dinner, Walker presented LeBron, Pittman, and Sutton with the framed jerseys and announced that they would be on display at the field. Then, Walker introduced LeBron. He stepped to the podium and the kids were silent. Their eyes were wide open. They concentrated on LeBron's every word, and LeBron knew he had a captive audience. He used that moment to discuss the importance of school. "Don't ever forget how important it is to do well in school," LeBron said. He ended his speech by saying, "Work hard in everything you do and remember to listen to your parents."

Being concerned for kids wasn't just a public relations move for LeBron. It just came naturally, probably because he'd

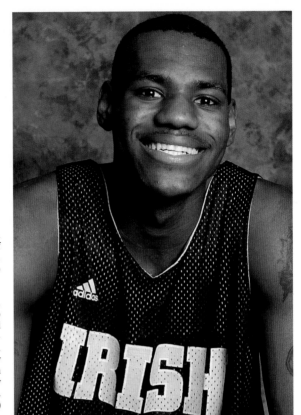

With a charismatic smile, LeBron knew how to be charming off the court. (Akron Beacon Journal, Phil Masturzo)

The "Fab Five"—Sian Cotton, LeBron, Dru Joyce III, Romeo Travis, and Willie McGee—stand tall and tough, flexing some muscle during their junior seasons. Maybe they were a bit too cocky here—this was the only year in their four-year careers that they didn't win the state title. (Akron Beacon Journal, Phil Masturzo)

When LeBron and the rest of the Irish basketball team arrived for a game, fans regularly mobbed the bus. (Akron Beacon Journal, Phil Masturzo)

After hearing about young Davonte Greer's horrific tragedy, LeBron wanted to help. The two became friends. (Akron Beacon Journal, Phil Masturzo)

In the state semifinal game his junior year, LeBron gets ready to make a strong baseline move to the basket against Poland Seminary. (Akron Beacon Journal, Phil Masturzo)

LeBron relaxes on the bench after the Irish win the regional championship his junior year, advancing to the state final four. (Akron Beacon Journal, Phil Masturzo)

"Heeeer's LeBron!" The Irish had a flair for the dramatic during pregame introductions, and the intros became somewhat of a spectacle. (Akron Beacon Journal, Phil Masturzo)

How often do most high school basketball teams check in at the airport on their way to a game? For St. Vincent-St. Mary, it became a common occurrence—infuriating Ohio High School Athletic Association commissioner Clair Muscaro. (Akron Beacon Journal, Phil Masturzo)

LeBron chows down in his hotel room while watching *SportsCenter* at night before a "road" game. (Akron Beacon Journal, Phil Masturzo)

Former NFL star Deion Sanders interviewed LeBron in Akron for a segment on the *CBS Early Show*. Sanders took a liking to the high school phenom. (Akron Beacon Journal, Phil Masturzo)

Fans get into the act during St. Vincent-St. Mary's nationally televised game on ESPN2. A documentary about LeBron aired following the game. (Akron Beacon Journal, Phil Masturzo)

The ESPN2 crew of Dick Vitale, Dan Schulman, and NBA Hall of Famer Bill Walton came to Cleveland for the St. Vincent-St. Mary–Oak Hill game. After the Irish beat the No. 1–ranked Oak Hill by 20 points, the LeBron hype machine was in high gear. (Akron Beacon Journal, Phil Masturzo)

In a touching show of support on Senior Night, LeBron's closest friends left their own parents' sides and walked out with LeBron because Gloria couldn't be there with him. It was another controversial moment that didn't need to be, if fans knew the real story. (Akron Beacon Journal, Phil Masturzo)

LeBron won the Ohio Associated Press "Mr. Basketball" award for an unprecedented three consecutive years. Here he poses for a newspaper story after receiving the award in his senior year.
(Akron Beacon Journal, Phil Masturzo)

There's LeBron's pride and joy, the Hummer. But LeBron flashes another sign of pride. It's an "A", for Akron. When the team played in California, the players came up with the sign to show people on the West Coast where they were from.

(Akron Beacon Journal, Phil Masturzo)

While the OHSAA was conducting its investigation into the ownership of the Hummer, LeBron decided to poke fun at the situation by driving a remote-control Hummer across the floor at Rhodes Arena during half-time of a junior varsity game. Inappropriate? Probably. But it certainly showed a sense of humor.

(Akron Beacon Journal, Phil Masturzo)

LeBron's liking for "throwback" jerseys, like the one he's wearing here, led to an OSHAA investigation that cost him his eligibility for two games his senior year. He was on the sidelines (looking more like a coach than a player, in his dapper suit) to support the team.
(Akron Beacon Journal, Phil Masturzo)

LeBron reacts to a call in the state championship his senior year that he felt should have gone St. Vincent-St. Mary's way.
(Akron Beacon Journal, Phil Masturzo)

The St. Vincent-St. Mary team poses together after winning the state championship—the school's third title in four years. (Patty Burdon)

After losing in the state title game during his junior year, LeBron refocused himself and led the team to another championship. The Fab Five ended their high school careers on top.
(Patty Burdon)

The EA Sports Roundball Classic, sponsored by Adidas and played at the United Center (home of the Chicago Bulls), was the second of three MVP postseason awards LeBron earned after his St. Vincent high school season was completed.
(Akron Beacon Journal, Phil Masturzo)

In the "sneaker war" over LeBron, Sonny Vacaro fought hard on behalf of Adidas, but LeBron walked away from that company's offer in favor of Nike. (Akron Beacon Journal, Phil Masturzo)

Although the St. Vincent-St. Mary team was supplied by Adidas, LeBron often wore Nike shoes with a custom inscription during his senior year. (Akron Beacon Journal, Phil Masturzo)

LeBron stands in front of the Michael Jordan statue at the United Center in Chicago. Jordan became something of a role model for LeBron throughout his high school years. (Patty Burdon)

Probably pondering the journey on which he is about to embark, LeBron tries to compose himself before making his big—though hardly surprising—announcement. (Akron Beacon Journal, Phil Masturzo)

Reporters from all over the U.S. converged on the St. Vincent-St. Mary campus when LeBron officially declared himself eligible for the 2003 NBA draft. (Akron Beacon Journal, Phil Masturzo)

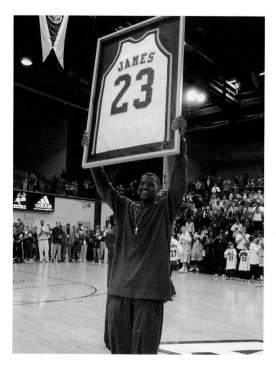

Only three basketball jerseys have been retired in the history of St. Vincent-St. Mary: those of former NBA forward Jerome Lane, former Ohio State point guard Curtis Wilson, and LeBron James. (Akron Beacon Journal, Phil Masturzo)

The Fab Five celebrate graduation. At St. Vincent-St. Mary, they were urged to earn good grades by teachers who cared more about learning and good citizenship than basketball. (Patty Burdon)

LeBron and Gloria share a tender moment in New York during the NBA draft.
(Akron Beacon Journal, Phil Masturzo)

Welcome to the
Millionaire's Club.
LeBron poses with NBA
commissioner David Stern
after the Cavaliers select
him as the No. 1 pick
in the 2003 draft.
(Akron Beacon Journal,
Phil Masturzo)

seen himself how tough life could get for kids and how generous people had been to him.

Even in small, offhand ways he seemed especially thoughtful for a guy who had yet to reach his 18th birthday.

Greg Nossaman said he would never forget the time LeBron made his son's night. Nossaman was the head coach at Willard High School, about an hour northwest of Akron. During the summer of LeBron's senior year, Willard and St. Vincent-St. Mary played each other in a scrimmage in Akron. At the time, LeBron wasn't playing because of an injury to his left wrist, which required a cast. Nossaman's son was a huge LeBron fan, and prior to the scrimmage, eight-year-old Nicklaus kept hinting to his dad that he wanted an autograph from LeBron. Finally, Nossaman walked over to LeBron, who was on the court and shooting balls with his right hand, and said, "LeBron, could you do me a favor? My son would really love an autograph. Would you sign one for him?" LeBron replied, "Coach, I'd love to, but I write with my left hand," he said, showing that the way the cast was fitted around his fingers made it almost impossible to write.

LeBron hated to see Nicklaus go away empty handed. "Coach, I'm sorry," he said. "But I'll do this, when you guys come back, I promise I'll give your son an autograph." LeBron looked down at Nicklaus, patted him on his head, and said, "Okay?"

Five months later, Nossaman brought his team back to Rhodes Arena for Willard's game against St. Vincent-St. Mary. LeBron, his left wrist healed, went up to the coach about an hour before the game and asked, "Is your son here?" He was. "I'd love to give him that autograph I promised; I can write now," as he held up his left wrist.

"I though it was really neat that LeBron remembered to do something like that from the summer," Nossaman said. "I didn't think anything of it. It just goes to show you the type of kid he is. He has a great heart."

It didn't appear to be the sort of act that LeBron had to think about; it was just the thing to do.

LeBron felt the same way when he heard about a local family that had suffered a terrible tragedy—affecting a woman and her young cousin.

On January 1, 2003, Demitra Greer, who lived on Akron's southwest side, lost three family members in a house fire. Greer's daughter, Mahogany, her 20-month-old granddaughter, Aniya, and her five-year-old niece, Sariya Stallings, were all killed in the fire. Apparently a pan was left on the stove inside the residence and smoke spread through the apartment. Witnesses said little Sariya managed to get out of the apartment initially, but ran back inside to help rescue her baby cousin. It was the ultimate act of heroism and bravery, and it cost the young girl her life. As firefighters made their way through the debris, they found Sariya in an upstairs hallway leading to the bedroom where baby Aniya was sleeping in her crib. Mahogany was found on the floor. Newspaper reports said that Sariya and her 9-year-old brother, Davonte Greer, were staying at the apartment with relatives because their mother was in the process of moving them into a new home. Davonte escaped the fire along with Mahogany's 8-year-old daughter, Tymesha.

After hearing about the tragedy, LeBron wanted to do something for the little boy and his family. The school, LeBron's family, and the Greers arranged for Davonte to attend a St. Vincent-St. Mary game, especially given the fact that LeBron was Davonte's favorite player—"of all time," he said. LeBron wanted to do more than just have Davonte come to the game. LeBron arranged for Davonte to take the bus from the school to Rhodes Arena, about a 10 minute ride. Davonte also was in the huddle when the players were introduced, and he sat on the bench during the game. During the postgame interviews, Davonte sat right next to his idol. After fielding a few questions about his record-setting game, LeBron introduced Davonte. "He's my new little man," LeBron said. "He's just like me, he's cool. He came through the huddle with us. He sat on the bench with us. If I can do anything to make him happy, I will."

Davonte, sporting a LeBron James T-shirt and a Nike headband during the postgame press conference, seemed somewhat overwhelmed by the media but took it all in stride and flashed a big smile. "It was fun," he said. Demitra was so happy to see the boy smiling again. "It's been really hard on us," she said, as her eyes filled with tears. She talked about how Davonte would come home from school and when he got off the bus, he would cry because he missed all of his relatives.

SEVENTEEN

CONTROVERSY

The greater his celebrity status grew, the more LeBron became a target—sometimes unfairly, sometimes with cause—
for the intense scrutiny and frequent moral judgments of the
news media and the general public. Throughout his senior
year in high school, LeBron seemed to ignite brush fires of
controversy wherever he went. Sometimes the controversy re-
sulted from factors he could hardly have controlled. Other
times, LeBron and his inner circle of family and friends clearly
helped fuel the fire.

One problem with "amateur" athletics is that it's hard to
agree on exactly what the term means. It's simple to say that in
amateur sports an athlete cannot be paid for playing. But what
is pay? It is common for schools to offer athletic scholarships,
for example. And many schools' athletic programs are sponsored—by anyone from a local business to Adidas—meaning
the kids might get up to several hundred dollars' worth of
equipment free. For some poorer schools, that's the only way
they can field a team in certain sports. The line between a per-
fectly acceptable amateur athletic program and one that takes
advantage of the athletes (or that the athletes themselves take
unfair advantage of) is invisible.

St. Vincent-St. Mary coaches and administrators were

being criticized—by outsiders and also by some within the
school's own community—for over-promoting the basketball
team. There was the complaint from Ohio High School Athletic Association commissioner Clair Muscaro about too much
travel. Muscaro further complained in the media that the
team's celebrity status was driving up ticket prices.

"I've heard from parents who have had to pay 12 to 15 dollars to see their son play just because they were playing against
St. Vincent-St. Mary," Muscaro said at a press conference.
"They're used to paying only three or four dollars, and now it's
like they're going to see a big-time college game. Is that fair?"

Some St. Vincent-St. Mary parents and alumni didn't like
that so many home games had been moved to the Rhodes
arena. School administrators countered that they had to move
the games to accommodate all the fans who wanted to attend;
they felt that the alternative—playing at home and leaving
many fans without tickets—would be worse. The players liked
their gym. It was comfortable and cozy, with the students in
the stands almost on top of the court. But the gym held only
1,700; it was old, and the bleachers creaked and shook with
each step.

"We have 600 kids, and if each kid brought a parent or two
you're already up to the number that our gym will hold," said
Joanne Zaratsian, the school's director of financial development.

The school had arranged for an overflow crowd to watch a
closed circuit broadcast, at no charge, in St. Vincent-St. Mary's
400-seat auditorium, but even that couldn't accommodate
everyone who wanted to watch.

So the cable company that was showing the closed circuit
feed, Time-Warner cable, suggested another solution: pay-
per-view broadcast, $7.95 per game, in the Akron area. The
school didn't make much money off the deal, but the public

didn't know that, and the general impression was that the school was cashing in.

LeBron didn't seem to pay much attention to the criticism of the school. But criticism of Gloria was hard to overlook.

Either Gloria's behavior in the stands at games grew more antic as LeBron's celebrity increased, or there were just more fans and reporters on hand to witness it. Either way, it drew attention—usually unfavorable.

Gloria had always been reluctant to talk to the media. Then, after a cover story about LeBron appeared in *ESPN The Magazine* that she thought had unfairly portrayed her in a negative light, she stopped talking to reporters almost entirely. So what most people knew of her came from what they saw in public.

In the stands at St. Vincent-St. Mary games, she was not shy about speaking her mind and showing her support for her son. It was the way she did that, though, that rankled many observers.

Gloria had been a factor at LeBron's games since he was a Pee Wee football player. One game, in particular, showed just how much Gloria's presence meant to him. LeBron's team, the South Rangers, were playing and had the ball for the first series of the game. Gloria had not arrived at the field yet, and LeBron noticed. On the first play, LeBron gained just a couple of yards. On the next two plays, he was tackled for a loss. The Rangers had to punt. While they were on defense, Gloria made her way to the sideline. When the Rangers got the ball back, LeBron scored on the first play—an 82-yard touchdown run. He scored again on the very next possession and finished with four touchdowns. On several of those long runs, Gloria was running right down the sideline with him, cheering him on.

"I remember that," LeBron later said, laughing a little embarrassedly. "She was always at my games and she was my biggest supporter. It was just a great feeling to have her there, because she has always been my best friend and nobody is like your mother—nobody."

"Glo is a very strong-minded person and she's misunderstood by a lot of people because people just really don't know her," Eddie Jackson said.

Gloria had earned her reputation for being a little over the top, to say the least.

In LeBron's junior year, during a game at the Cleveland State University Convocation Center against Brush (Ohio), she got into a shouting match with the mother and other family members of a Brush player. The brush player fouled LeBron hard while LeBron was going up for a dunk. When LeBron hit the ground underneath the basket, Gloria, who typically sat right behind the St. Vincent-St. Mary bench, jumped out of her seat and was ready to run out on the court before being restrained. (It was a few games later in that season when she actually did go on the court during the game against George Junior Republic.)

When St. Vincent-St. Mary played against Philadelphia's Strawberry Mansion High School high school at the University of Pennsylvania's legendary Palestra during LeBron's senior year, Gloria nearly caused a riot.

High school basketball in the Philadelphia area is huge. Wilt Chamberlain played prep basketball in the Philly area; so did Kobe Bryant. Fans in Philadelphia couldn't wait to see hometown hero Maureece Rice, who broke Chamberlain's Philadelphia high school all-time scoring mark, show LeBron and the Irish what real East Coast high school basketball was all about. Instead, the 8,722 fans at the Palestra saw Rice and Strawberry Mansion, the defending Philadelphia Public

League champs, get dismantled by St. Vincent-St. Mary 85-47, as LeBron scored 26 points, grabbed eight rebounds, dished out five assists, and had seven steals.

With the game already decided at halftime, Gloria, who as usual wore a replica St. Vincent-St. Mary game jersey with "LeBron's Mom" on the back, started to taunt and antagonize the crowd because the game was already a blowout. The fans started to boo Gloria, but she didn't care because her babies (she talked about everyone on the team like they were her kids) were getting the job done.

Then there was the game against Mentor (Ohio), at Rhodes Arena. LeBron scored 50 points in that game, which was a blowout. Before game time, family friend Chris Dennis was passing out hand-held fans with LeBron's picture on the front. After LeBron finally was taken out of the game, Gloria went over to the opposing stands holding one of the LeBron fans above her head, letting the Mentor faithful know who was No. 1. The Mentor fans started booing Gloria. Far from minding the boos, she actually seemed to enjoy them.

Friends figured, that's just Gloria—she doesn't care what anybody thinks, especially when it comes to her son, and she'd do anything she needed to do to protect him.

Most high school kids are readily embarrassed by their parents—whatever their behavior. LeBron never let Gloria's behavior—or people's criticism of her—bother him. "I know people think my mother is loud and stuff like that," LeBron said. "But I love her to death. She's like my sister, my mother, my father, and my brother."

While her behavior was easy to criticize, many who criticized it didn't know much about Gloria's background. They didn't know that she had raised her son without the support of a mother, a father, a grandmother, a husband, or any substantial income. For most of her life she'd had nothing—except

LeBron. From day one, nobody would have given her much of a chance to succeed even with him.

Now, with LeBron clearly on the verge of success that would lead to their financial independence for the very first time, she felt like she was running the show. Finally, she would be the one calling the shots instead of having to rely on others. Some people suggested that she would be more liked if she just softened her demeanor and tried to shed the negative, hard image. But Gloria wouldn't change her personality just to please other people. Her life had been rough, and she never made excuses; she took what life dished out because she had no choice. Now, it would be her turn, and she'd do things her own way, whether people liked it or not.

Eddie could be just as much a character as Gloria. He was known to be loud and vocal during LeBron's games at St. Vincent-St. Mary. In fact, one time during LeBron's junior year he had to be escorted out of Rhodes Arena by five Akron police officers. The Irish were playing archrival Archbishop Hoban in a sold-out game. In Northeast Ohio high school basketball, this was a rivalry as heated as that of the Cleveland Browns–Pittsburgh Steelers.

St. Vincent-St. Mary supporters didn't like the fact that the Knights came out during pregame warmups wearing T-shirts with "The Chosen One" on them—a play on the *Sports Illustrated* cover. Hoban fans, on the other hand, were upset with the verbal abuse by the Irish faithful—including Eddie. Eddie was upset because he thought the Hoban coach had sent in a player to go after LeBron. The reserve player, who looked like a college football player, committed two or three hard fouls against LeBron in the span of a few minutes. Eddie got out of his seat, which was in the first row at Rhodes Arena near the

Irish Bench, and walked over behind Hoban's bench, in direct ear-shot of the coach. Not a good idea.

Eddie caused such a scene that one of the officers there to provide security tried to calm him down and get him back to his seat. But Eddie, who'd had past encounters with the police, got more irate that the officer was instructing him to sit down. The police officer made a call for help, and quickly several other officers grabbed Eddie and escorted him out of the arena. Eddie wasn't arrested, but it caused a big scene. After that game, the two teams, which had played one another for years, decided to end the basketball rivalry for a while.

Some people grumbled about Gloria and Eddie, complaining that the two boisterous fans had only lately become interested in attending LeBron's games—after they realized that there would be a big payday in the young man's future. But anyone who had attended LeBron's early games, from the Pee Wee football or AAU basketball days, would have noticed that Gloria and Eddie were there—you couldn't miss them.

EIGHTEEN

THE HUMMER

Gloria and Eddie were central figures in the controversy that became northeast Ohio's biggest unimportant sports story of the year 2002: The Hummer.

The Hummer was hard not to notice.

The huge, platinum/silver Hummer H2 sport-utility vehicle had a base price of $53,000. But that was before the accessories. The DVD player, three televisions, PlayStation 2, sparkling rims, full leather interior with custom "King James" logos, and other features probably brought the price closer to $80,000. That was more—far more—than the price of a house on some of the streets where LeBron and Gloria had lived.

Sure, many high school kids get a car for their 18th birthday. But not one like this. And not from a mom without a job, on welfare, living in subsidized housing.

By December 2002, though, everybody in Akron knew that LeBron was headed toward a lucrative NBA contract within months. And though Gloria was unemployed, simply being the beloved mother of LeBron James gave her Blue Chip capital.

"It was something we wanted to get for him, period, regardless of what the media thought. This kid deserved it, and to hell with what everybody else thought," Eddie said later.

The Hummer purchase might have been written off by

many as just a garish display by a soon-to-be-*nouveau-riche* sports star. It was an almost mind-boggling amount of money to spend on a gift, but then again, when you have the means to do something nice for someone you love, who is to criticize?

Quite a lot of people, as it turned out.

The Ohio High School Athletic Association, the governing body for high school athletics, had a rule stating that an athlete would forfeit his or her amateur standing by "capitalizing on athletic fame by receiving money or gifts of monetary value."

As word got out that LeBron was driving around Akron in a glitzy new car, the OHSAA office in Columbus began receiving phone calls.

The organization took the Hummer matter very seriously.

"When our member schools see something like that, it throws up a red flag," OHSAA commissioner Clair Muscaro said. "It's different than a parent buying their son or daughter a small vehicle. If there is any chance that it [the Hummer] was provided by an agent, he would immediately lose his eligibility, and as far as we're concerned, that would be when he accepted the car. Once a player loses his amateur status, if he plays after that, his team would have to forfeit those games."

St. Vincent-St. Mary officials had already looked into the matter and satisfied themselves that LeBron remained eligible. Athletic Director Grant Innocenzi explained that they would cooperate fully. The school, though, was not the target of the investigation.

Muscaro's job was to follow the financial paper trail in regard to the Hummer, and to make sure it ended at Gloria or Eddie. But Muscaro didn't get the proper paperwork he needed promptly, and his investigation dragged out over weeks.

When Gloria and Eddie weren't immediately forthcoming with answers, most people assumed it was because the answers would create more trouble.

It's doubtful that LeBron truly understood what he was facing by getting a luxury sports utility vehicle in the middle of the basketball season. "I did ask LeBron if he was ready (for the criticism), and I told him that I didn't want him whining and crying when it happened," said Coach Dru Joyce II. "I don't think LeBron knew how some people would view it, because he's only 18. Like a lot of us, the school would have preferred this hadn't happened, but this was Gloria's decision. She believes she has the right to buy her son this kind of gift, and she does. She would not want to do anything that would cause LeBron or the other players any trouble (with the OHSAA). It's not like it came from Nike or something. It was a birthday gift from his mother. Parents buy kids cars for their 18th birthdays all the time and they play on teams, and they aren't investigated."

Gloria and Eddie may have been guilty of poor timing of the purchase, but at least they did their homework. "We checked with everybody we needed to before the vehicle was purchased to make sure LeBron's eligibility wouldn't be jeopardized," Eddie said.

Their boy was turning 18 in December 2002. He had maintained good grades at a good school in the midst of national celebrity and the endless calls from television shows, radio shows, print media reporters, and motion picture producers. He had focused on his team, spending practice seeing how everyone could work together for the good of all, not showboating or bragging about his future. It was obvious that he was going to go professional when he graduated from high school. He had worked hard, done well, and was a rich young man waiting to happen.

They thought he deserved something special for his 18th birthday.

Insiders in the professional sports world know that it's not uncommon for financial institutions to give loans to college athletes in their senior year when it becomes clear they will become top professional draft choices.

The dealer Eddie and Gloria bought the car from was 310 Motoring Automobile Specialists of Los Angeles, which specialized in sales to celebrities—NBA stars like Kobe Bryant, Kevin Garnett, and Antoine Walker; entertainers like Denzel Washington, Jennifer Lopez, and Britney Spears. The Hummer was actually one of the less expensive and least ostentatious makes they sold. The dealer was a good choice for a customer who wanted details kept out of the newspapers, and they were familiar with the financing requirements of top-prospect athletes and Hollywood types—such as paying very little money down and having unusually low payments per month until the draft was over, the record was released, or the movie deal was completed.

Around Akron, kids and even grownups would spot LeBron's Hummer, see the 310 Motoring trademark on the license plate, and follow the vehicle. Through the tinted windows, you couldn't actually see who was driving. As it rolled through Akron, the Hummer represented many things—mystery, intrigue, envy. When LeBron pulled up to a red light and someone pulled next to him, you could read people's lips. "Is that LeBron?" And on many occasions, it wasn't, because LeBron and Gloria were generous about letting close friends drive the Hummer.

Some of the sports reporters even claimed to have noticed more Hummers on the road in the Akron area after LeBron received his. (Trying to capitalize on the controversy, a Cleveland-area Hummer dealership ran radio ads encouraging listeners to buy the car that LeBron was now driving.)

It's interesting that the Hummer wasn't actually the first luxury automobile LeBron received from Gloria and Eddie. For a while during his junior year, LeBron was regularly seen driving a newer-model Lincoln Navigator, which, at the time, was considered by teens to be the mother of all sports utility vehicles. The Navigator wasn't as fully-equipped as the Hummer, but it was sweet. Nobody got upset with that vehicle, perhaps because it was used and there were many others on the road so it didn't stand out quite so much. It was owned by Eddie.

While OSHAA and the media scrutinized the Hummer purchase—what details they could find, at least—criticized his mother in the news, and followed him to get a picture of his flashy new car, LeBron tried not to let it bother him. It certainly didn't seem to affect his game. (The St. Vincent-St. Mary team was still playing basketball, after all.) At the first game after the Hummer controversy broke, played in Rhodes Arena against Mentor, he was ready to go from tipoff. Just 15 seconds into the game, LeBron threw down a nasty reverse dunk, and it was just a sign of things to come. He scored 50 points (a school record at the time) on 19-of-25 shooting from the field and also set a school record with 11 three-pointers as St. Vincent-St. Mary clobbered Mentor 92-56.

Before the game, LeBron even pulled a little prank to let off some steam.

At halftime of the junior varsity game that preceded the varsity game, LeBron went to center court and started to play with a remote-control Hummer. He set the toy down, and then maneuvered it all over the court. His actions drew chuckles from the crowd, but some felt he was mocking Muscaro and the OHSAA. Only those who knew LeBron knew he wasn't mocking the authorities; instead, he was making light of the entire situation.

"He was poking fun right back at you guys [the media]," said Sonny Vaccaro, the head of Adidas, who was closely watching the situation. "He had all the pressure in the world.

They wanted to kill this kid, and he's out there playing with the Hummer. That was smart, and it shows you that this kid is aware of his surroundings."

Coach Joyce took some heat for letting it happen, but said he was unaware of what LeBron was going to do until he was already out on the court. "Maybe I let it go on longer than I should have," he said.

Gloria finally set the Hummer matter to rest by sharing the details of the purchase with the *Akron Beacon Journal.* She explained that she and Eddie had checked first to make sure the gift wouldn't jeopardize LeBron, and told how the loan was handled. The story ran in the paper, and about a week later, after Muscaro felt he had sufficient documentation, he concluded the OSHAA investigation. He issued a one-page statement that said the transaction was not a violation of the OHSAA bylaws on amateurism.

Coach Dru was one who thought the timing of the gift was bad, but he respected Gloria's decision. "I truly believed right from the start that everything on Gloria's part was done right and she assured me that they had done the research and that they looked into everything," he said. "I knew she wouldn't do anything to jeopardize LeBron and the kids."

Several days passed. Athletic director Grant Innocenzi was glad to have the hysteria behind him. All he had to do was prepare the gym for that night's game. But the Hummer wouldn't go away.

First came a call from the school's headmaster, Dave Rathz. There was a Hummer parked on the sidewalk, blocking the walkway.

"When I got the call on my radio, I knew exactly who to go to," Innocenzi said, with a huge smile on his face. He found

LeBron a few minutes later. "LeBron, you gotta move your car, man."

LeBron replied, "Mr. Innocenzi, I couldn't find a parking spot, plus somebody was messing with it."

When LeBron left school that Friday, his thoughts may have been on the upcoming game but they were not on the road. Though accomplished on the basketball court, LeBron was average, at best, behind the wheel. He drove up Maple Street Hill and stopped at a red light at West Market Street. Directly behind him was 88-year-old Iola Winston in her 2000 Dodge Stratus. She sat patiently. He rolled backwards. The two cars met. The Hummer won.

"I asked him why he backed into me, and he said he didn't see me," Iola Winston told the police. "He asked for my telephone number and [said] that he would have someone fix it, and he got in his car and left."

Iola Winston was upset and confused by the incident. The tall driver had been quite nice, but her car was damaged and she realized she needed to have the accident on the record. She left where they had struck one another and called the police. However, she did not file a full report until her brother convinced her to do so. This she did three days later, assuring that the insurance company would be satisfied—and also bringing the incident to the media's attention.

Aha! LeBron and the Hummer in trouble again. This time, the controversy petered out quickly.

"It's a civil matter and both parties made agreements," the police explained when called for comment.

Iola Winston was satisfied when LeBron handled his responsibility. "His insurance took care of everything and they fixed my car," she said, later.

"He was a nice kid. I think he was nervous."

NINETEEN

JERSEY TROUBLE

Eddie Jackson, the man LeBron called his father, had become an ever more important part of LeBron's life during the boy's adolescent years. But he had not been there for LeBron, at least physically, during the Hummer incident. And he wouldn't be there for the rest of LeBron's senior year. He would miss walking out onto the court with LeBron for St. Vincent-St. Mary's Senior Night. He would miss watching LeBron win a state and national championship. He would miss graduation and miss the celebration of LeBron's selection in the NBA draft.

Eddie, referred to in the media as LeBron's "surrogate father," wasn't there for any of it, and it pained him deeply—because it was all his fault. Eddie was back in jail. He was serving a three-year sentence in the Federal Correctional Facility in Loretto, Pennsylvania, after pleading guilty in late August of 2002 to federal bank and mail fraud charges—for obtaining a mortgage with false documents and opening a bank account with a stolen check.

His lawyer said in court that Eddie's crimes were "hard to justify," and that "it seems that whenever Eddie goes back to drinking, he makes bad decisions." Unfortunately, those bad decisions hurt other people—especially LeBron.

"Mere words alone cannot express nor explain how proud I

am of that kid," Eddie said from prison, his voice soft, his words meaningful and strong. "I would die, and come back to life again, then die again and come back to life again and still wouldn't be able to come up with enough words to explain how proud I am of him. It hurts not seeing all my kids . . . LeBron, La'Shell, and Taylor [Eddie's biological children from other relationships], it hurts every day. LeBron knows I'm there with him mentally and spiritually."

Most people who knew him considered Eddie to be basically a good guy. When he met you at a game, or on the street, or at the YMCA during an afternoon pick-up basketball game, he was polite, respectful, and fun to be around. He wasn't the kind of guy who went looking for trouble. But somehow trouble always seemed to find him, and he apparently didn't try hard enough to resist it.

Eddie wanted to make sure LeBron didn't follow in his footsteps, though.

"I made sure that he didn't do the things I did," Eddie said. "We protected him and made sure he was around the right people who would prevent him from making the mistakes that some of us did."

In an interview from his prison cell he said, "It hurts when people say that me or Gloria failed as parents, because I know we made mistakes, but we love that boy. It hurts when I hear Dick Vitale saying things like LeBron needs to be careful of his surroundings, as if everyone around him are total failures. I'm very happy and comfortable with every single person who is out there and around him. I have not been failed by none, in my opinion. All of them stepped up and did a wonderful job protecting LeBron and his image."

Maybe so, but a trip to prison by his father figure was just the sort of thing LeBron and his image needed protection from.

Eddie thought that racial and cultural differences made

many people think less of him than he deserved. "Some whites don't understand the [black] culture, even more so, they don't understand that we were supposed to be an atypical family. I wasn't supposed to be LeBron's father and people hated seeing Gloria doing and saying what she felt. The media made us look dysfunctional," Eddie said.

Eddie, as a convicted felon, was fair game in the media. However, in press reports about Eddie's conviction, his relationship with LeBron was usually mentioned—with LeBron's name often prominent. The reports always made it clear that LeBron had no connection to Eddie's crimes, but to many who read them these news reports themselves seemed to exploit the teenager.

The *Akron Beacon Journal* received many angry letters and email messages from readers after the paper ran several stories about Eddie's legal troubles.

"Taking advantage of LeBron James' basketball stardom to catapult Eddie Jackson, Jr. to front-page status . . . was an opportunist folly," said one letter to the editor.

"Your articles certainly have robbed LeBron of his innocence," wrote another reader.

"This is exploitation," said a third. "He's still a kid and there is no reason to include his name in those stories."

The newspaper responded to the complaints in an article about the criticism that ran in the paper. "We have tried to be sensitive to this issue," David Hertz, the editor in charge of local news coverage, was quoted as saying. "However, when the person who advises LeBron James on his financial future is charged with fraud, that's news by any journalistic standard."

Newspaper and television reports about LeBron had for months been filled with symbols of success and hints of corruption—high school players jetting around the country for their games, stepping in and out of limousines; an ultra-flashy car; a mentor sent off to prison. Yet LeBron seemed to take every controversy in stride. So it came as a surprise that what nearly finished him were three shirts worth $845. Ironically, it wound up leading to a positive experience for his teammates.

LeBron and his friends liked what were called "throwback" jerseys, replicas of athletic jerseys once worn by ballplayers who had retired or moved to other teams. Early in his senior year, LeBron was noticed during post-game press conferences wearing a New Orleans Saints jersey with Jim Everette's name or a San Diego Chargers jersey with Lance Alworth's name.

LeBron and his friends had come to Cleveland to watch a basketball game between two suburban teams, Warrensville Heights and Shaker Heights, then stopped at a fashionable clothing store called Next Urban Gear, to browse. The customers were often young, hip, and famous. Rapper Ja Rule relied on Next for some of his clothing whenever he was in Cleveland. Shaquille O'Neal shopped at Next, as did former Cleveland Browns football stars Corey Fuller and Earl Little, former Indians player Kenny Lofton, and numerous other individuals in the worlds of music, entertainment, and sports. The walls were adorned with photos of famous customers

LeBron knew Joe Hathorn, the man in charge of the store. Hathorn was a friend of Eddie's and had followed LeBron's career like everyone else connected with basketball and sports in northeastern Ohio.

When the friends were done browsing, LeBron went to Hathorn to say goodbye. Hathorn impulsively handed him a present of two throwback jerseys—a Wes Unseld and a Gale Sayers.

LeBron reportedly replied, "You don't have to do that, but thank you."

Accepting the gift turned out to be a big mistake. The jerseys, which ran a total of $845 if bought retail, violated the rules for high school athletes.

The store owner, who was involved in Project LEARN, a nonprofit adult literacy organization, later stated that he knew LeBron had made the honor roll and had wanted to reward him for being a good student. A newspaper report suggested instead that LeBron received the clothing in exchange for his posing for pictures that were to be hung on a wall.

OHSAA commissioner Clair Muscaro, who had not been able to find any irregularities surrounding LeBron's new Hummer, must have thought he finally had LeBron this time. Just four days after concluding his Hummer investigation and one day after hearing about the jerseys, Muscaro announced in a public statement that a violation of the OHSAA amateur bylaws had been found, and that, therefore, he ruled LeBron ineligible for the remainder of his high school career. Also, St. Vincent-St. Mary would have to forfeit its recent game against Akron Buchtel, because LeBron had played in that game after forfeiting his amateur status.

"In talking with the store's personnel," Muscaro said in his statement, "I was able to confirm that on January 25 the merchant gave the clothing directly to LeBron at no cost. This is a direct violation of the OHSAA bylaws on amateurism, because, in fact, LeBron did capitalize on athletic fame by receiving these gifts."

LeBron was crushed.

Gloria felt he had been treated unfairly.

"None of us was even notified by OHSAA that an investigation was under way, much less permitted to provide any information," Gloria said. "We do not understand how this could be considered a fair process."

During the Hummer controversy, she had gotten the help

of a high-profile Cleveland lawyer, Fred Nance—managing partner of the large law firm of Squires, Sanders and Dempsey. Now, Nance set to work trying to keep LeBron playing while a legal challenge to the OSHAA jersey ruling was mounted.

Nance's presence in the controversy raised more money questions. How was Gloria able to retain such a high-priced lawyer? But Nance was well known and highly respected in the community; clearly either he was glad to help out in hope of landing a valuable future client, or concerned about helping a decent kid like LeBron whom he thought was getting unfair treatment, or a little of both. Either way, LeBron definitely needed the help.

Nance, on LeBron's behalf, claimed that the store owner had given the jerseys as a reward for *academic* performance, not because of basketball. Perhaps more believable was his complaint that Muscaro's ruling was arbitrary and capricious because Muscaro did not conduct a thorough investigation. Nance accused Muscaro of succumbing to public pressure following his ruling about the Hummer. Muscaro acted as "prosecutor, judge, and jury in what can only be considered an ill-advised and ill-motivated decision," Nance asserted.

The key points Nance argued in legal papers were:

Muscaro did not notify LeBron of the investigation.

Muscaro did not provide LeBron with notice of the charges against him.

Muscaro did not provide LeBron any hearing with regard to the allegations. This would have allowed LeBron the opportunity to present witnesses on his behalf.

Muscaro did not provide LeBron an opportunity to tell his side of the story.

In response, Muscaro told the Associated Press that he asked school administrators for a chance to speak with James. "But LeBron did not want to speak with me."

The news that the top high school player in the country had been declared ineligible spread like wildfire. Local television stations had a crawl at the bottom of the screen announcing the news. ESPN ran big with the story. A few hours after the ruling, television trucks were parked all along the street outside the high school as members of the basketball team, including LeBron, were trying to get inside the building for practice. One man stood on the sidewalk with a paper bag over his head, trying to conceal his identity, but he was holding up a big sign that read, "Free LeBron." The fact that LeBron was not arrested for anything, had not committed a crime, and was not accused of a crime seemed irrelevant to the emotional hype.

Nance filed for a temporary restraining order against the OHSAA ruling, to allow LeBron to keep playing while the ruling was disputed.

Some onlookers suggested that the legal proceedings were pointless, that LeBron should just move on and turn pro, like he would in a matter of weeks anyway.

"He has had some well-known professional athletes saying, 'Why put up with the aggravation? Let it go and just start your [professional] career,'" Nance said. "He didn't consider that for a heartbeat. He's about finishing his season and winning a state championship and getting his team the No. 1 national ranking. That's what makes him tick."

Nance made LeBron aware of the risk he was taking by continuing to play. "LeBron has the very real potential to earn millions, potentially tens of millions," Nance said. "He's doing all of this because he doesn't want to let his teammates, his school, or himself down with the goals he's set. He's doing it at the risk of even one year as a professional that could set him financially for life. That speaks to the character of the young man."

The OSHAA ruling meant LeBron would have to miss playing in a high school game for the first time in his career. That was the Sunday game at Rhodes Arena against Ohio's perennial Division I power Canton McKinley. Coach Dru announced that LeBron would not play and he would not practice with the team. He was respecting Muscaro's ruling while the appeal was pending.

Speaking to reporters before his team took the court that Friday, Coach Dru looked perplexed and dejected. He knew the decision took its toll on team morale, but "We are a team, we'll play as a team and I believe in this team," he said. "I talked to the team collectively, and LeBron is part of the team, and I explained to them that sometimes in your life you have to take responsibility for your actions and you have to make the most out of it and move on."

Privately, LeBron was distraught. "I'm sorry. There's nothing I'm more sorry about, you know, than disrespecting my teammates," he said. "I love them to death. . . . I'm so proud of them, you know, to be able to stick it out for me."

Little Dru and the rest of the team didn't judge LeBron or hold any grudges against him because they knew the real LeBron and knew he would never have done anything, willingly, to jeopardize himself or the team.

The St. Vincent-St. Mary team would have to defend its No. 1 national ranking without its best player.

The day before the game, the Irish practiced at the school. There were no television camera crews around. Just the players, the coaching staff, a few supporters, and friends like Maverick Carter and Frankie Walker, Jr., who were often at the gym watching practice. LeBron was there, but he wasn't dressed in his usual Irish practice gear. He had on his own tank top and shorts. He was shooting around with the team, throwing down vicious reverse dunks and just clowning around until Coach Joyce blew the whistle and practice officially started. Then LeBron rolled the ball to the center of the court and somberly walked over to the bench to sit with his friends on the sideline.

Maverick had brought a few fast-food breakfast sandwiches and orange juices. LeBron, still sweating from his workout on the court, reached his hand into the bag to grab a sandwich. He slowly opened the wrapper, looked up at his friends, and said, "This is crazy. I took the jerseys back. I just want to play."

LeBron was right, but he had handled it wrong. He waited until the day he was ruled ineligible before returning the jerseys to the store. Whether things would have gone better had he returned them the moment the gift was questioned is unknown. But he waited, and it was too late.

LeBron stayed for the entire practice, never leaving the bench. St. Vincent-St. Mary had played 95 consecutive games with LeBron in the lineup, dating back to his freshman season when the Irish went 27-0 and won the Division III state championship. Looking back over the teams they defeated that year—Oak Hill; Mater Dei from Santa Ana, California; Philadelphia Strawberry Mansion; Los Angeles West Chester; R. J. Reynolds from North Carolina—clearly this was one of, it not the best team in the country.

Still, how good was this team without LeBron?

The Saturday game should have belonged to LeBron. Former NFL star "Neon" Deion Sanders was there to interview LeBron for the *CBS Early Show*. But now while the rest of the team was on the court, LeBron was sitting on the bench in street clothes.

The game, even without LeBron, seemed to belong to the Irish. The team had worked together in the past, though

LeBron frequently dominated the shooting. Tonight, though, it was Little Dru, the great outside shooter who had been kept in the background since the AAU days, who took command. Dru, the small point guard who averaged 12 points a game, that night took shots he might normally have passed off to LeBron. He finished with 21 points, and the Irish won, 63-62.

No one was more delighted with Little Dru and his performance than LeBron. What mattered even more was that the Irish won without LeBron. They played brilliantly together. The seniors had proven themselves in ways that no one would have believed had LeBron been on the court with them.

Legal wrangling continued over the OHSAA ruling. Nance's temporary restraining order request was filed and the case was assigned to common pleas court.

A press conference was held at St. Vincent-St. Mary so the high school's executive board could officially give LeBron its support. "LeBron did nothing that would justify the decision by the OHSAA to suspend his eligibility," said James Burdon, chairman of the executive board of trustees and an Akron lawyer. "The consequences are so severe, it's far disproportionate to the conduct and our support of LeBron is because of who he is. He's a member of the school community here. In his years as a student, he has excelled academically and socially, as well as athletically. As part of our school community, he deserves our wholehearted support."

LeBron even had support from the Akron City Council, which had voted unanimously to ask the OHSAA to reconsider the ruling. "I think LeBron needs to know this community supports him," Council President Marco Sommerville said. "Somewhere along the line, we need to understand he's just a kid."

LeBron returned to the team to play against Los Angeles West Chester in the Prime Time Shoot Out at Sovereign Bank Arena in Trenton, New Jersey. The game was a LeBron James classic.

He scored a school-record and career high 52 points for a 78-52 win in front of a sellout crowd of 8,500. He seemed to do little wrong all evening. He scored 18 of St. Vincent-St. Mary's 20 first-quarter points, and when the Irish were ahead 41-24, LeBron had scored 31 of those points. And the opposing Westchester team was ranked No. 7 in the country with two outstanding players—Trevor Azira, a UCLA recruit, and Scott Cutley, a Kent State University recruit.

Late in the third quarter, LeBron stole a pass and finished the play with a dunk, which prompted Westchester to call an immediate timeout. The dunk brought the crowd to its feet, and as James was about to walk off the court toward the bench, ball boy Jovan Marino ran onto the court and jumped right into LeBron's arms, and the star basketball player gave the little guy a hug.

"I just jumped up in his arms like he was my dad," said Marino. "It was like he gave me a present."

The Irish had two more games before LeBron's hearing on his eligibility, but one was cancelled because of inclement weather. The state high school tournament started the following week, and Coach Joyce didn't want LeBron sit out a tournament game, so he came up with some creative scheduling. He managed to schedule a game for the day before the tournament began, against Akron Firestone, whose head coach was happy for the opportunity. "Heck, we'll show up to play the Lakers," he said.

Firestone would receive a $7,500 check from St. Vincent-St.

Mary for the trouncing they received, even without LeBron playing.

Though he sat out the game as his second suspension, it was still LeBron's day, as his jersey was retired during a postgame ceremony. The school had previously retired the jerseys of guard Curtis Wilson, who later starred at Ohio State, and Jerome Lane, who once led the nation in rebounding at Pitt and played in the NBA with Denver and Cleveland. LeBron's jersey was hung in the gymnasium after he graduated.

"We thought about all the things that we could do to honor LeBron, and we felt retiring LeBron's jersey during the last game of the season was the best idea," Grant Innocenzi said. "We also thought about waiting until next year, but there was no guarantee he'd be able to come back."

Finally, three months after "Jerseygate" began, the judge finally rendered his decision. He dismissed LeBron's lawsuit against the Ohio High School Athletic Association but said the school did not have to forfeit any games or the state championship title. Judge Williams also barred the OHSAA from taking further action against the school.

His coach was proud of the way LeBron handled himself throughout the Hummer and jersey incidents.

"I have great respect for LeBron because of all that he has been through and the way that he has carried himself through all this," Coach Dru said. "There were a lot of things that happened that honestly, most kids his age would not have been able to handle, but he handled it very well, and all those things that a lot of people meant for evil, God turned them to good."

LeBron stood tall, even after all of the scrutiny. "Maybe some people would say, why me? I don't look at it that way. I've been through adversity my whole life, from moving from place to place and living in different environments so adversity was nothing new to me. Blaming other people is the easy way out. I blame myself. I'm glad it was me because it made me a better person. It made me stronger."

TWENTY

FRIENDS TO THE END

Based on all the media hype, public acclaim, and controversy heaped on LeBron throughout his senior year at St. Vincent-St. Mary, someone looking back on the period might easily assume that his teammates were merely onlookers with especially good seats at the LeBron James Show.

Anyone who was familiar with the team knew otherwise.

This team would go down as one of the best in Ohio high school history, and its core, the Fab Five—LeBron, Dru, Willie, Sian, and Romeo—won three state titles in four years. Their senior year, they were ranked No. 1 in the nation by *USA Today* in the country's most recognized high school sports poll. No single player could make a basketball team that good for that long.

And to LeBron, this team meant much more than just basketball.

LeBron loved his mother. LeBron found the father he was lacking in Eddie. But his brothers LeBron found on the basketball court. Theirs was a story about playing well and winning big, sure, but most of all it was a story about five boys from varying backgrounds who came together as best friends—and intended to stay that way forever.

One outsider who got an extraordinary inside look at the

team was Kris Belman, then a 23-year-old senior film major at Loyola Marymount University in Los Angeles. For a documentary class he was taking, Belman, an Akron native, wanted to make a film about the St. Vincent-St. Mary basketball team.

He received permission from the school to film the documentary but also needed to get permission from the team's coach. Coach Dru didn't want any more distractions. The team had way too many already. Yet surprisingly he okayed the idea anyway, because after meeting with Belman he realized the young man wasn't just planning a LeBron tribute; he was doing a project about the *team*.

Granted special access, the young film student with his hand-held camera filmed the team during pregame warmups. He filmed the team from the bench during the game. He was in the locker room, on the bus, in the hotel rooms, and he saw what no one else saw.

"During the time I spent with the team, I got a chance to see that they are just regular kids," Belman said. "I would say that the biggest misconception that everyone seems to have is that LeBron isn't having fun. Everyone grilled him, but he just wanted to be a kid. When he was with his team, it was like they were all a big family."

During the state championship game against Dayton Kettering, the Fab Five's final game together, Belman was able to capture the emotions of the team from the time they boarded the bus from its hotel in Columbus to the time the bus arrived at Ohio State's Value City Arena. His camera was rolling during the 15-minute ride. No one said a word on the bus. It was absolutely quiet. LeBron, Dru, Sian, and many other players had their headphones over their ears and their hoods on. They were in their own little worlds.

As game time slowly approached, Coach Joyce began his pregame speech.

"I hope you realize what you guys have a chance to do," he said, in a calm, soft voice. LeBron, sitting in one corner of the locker room, was wearing his customary NBA headband and chewing his gum intensely. He was staring at the floor listening as Coach Dru talked. Romeo had his hands clasped together as if he were praying. Sian was looking right into Coach Dru's mouth. "You have a chance to go down as one of the greatest boys high school basketball teams in the history of Ohio basketball, and you can't piss this opportunity away. You know, this is bigger than you guys." Coach Joyce then turned to the chalkboard to go over strategies for the game. He looked at the board for a few seconds. The locker room was silent. That brief moment seemed like an eternity. He then turned around and said, "Forget all of this stuff up here. Forget about it. This is all about what's inside here," he said, pumping his fist to his chest, with so much emotion and passion. "It's all about heart." Coach Joyce gathered himself and left his team with these words. "Fellas, you just have to go out there and leave everything out on the court."

They did just that, and followed their hearts to one final championship.

Their most emotional moment, though, came several weeks earlier, on Senior Night—in the midst of the Hummer controversy. Anyone who wanted to know what being teammates and best friends meant to these youngsters would have seen it all then.

At Senior Night, the senior classmen of St. Vincent-St. Mary's team would be specially honored, along with their families, before the game. The boys had requested that this game be played not at the Rhodes Arena but at the St. Vincent-St. Mary gym, because that was home and this game was special.

The day of that game was the same day LeBron had his accident in the Hummer. Because a police report had not been taken at the crash site, LeBron would have to file paperwork to comply with the state's financial responsibility laws. Otherwise the accident could have cost him his license and a substantial fine. However, because of his age, Gloria could go on his behalf and show proof that LeBron was fully insured. She was worried that if LeBron had to take care of the paperwork, he might be late for the Senior Night game. Gloria would have none of that. She sent him on without her.

At the gym, the junior varsity game was already on while Gloria was handling the police papers and insurance work needed to ensure that the accident would be handled properly. The large ceremony for the graduating seniors connected with the basketball team was going to take place between the junior varsity and the varsity games. All the parents were in place except Gloria, and soon people were talking about her in the gym.

Gloria was known for her tendency to make a dramatic entrance—considered "fashionably late" by some and "rude" by others. That night, though, of all nights, it was felt that LeBron needed his mother to show up on time.

Gloria, though, was taking care of business.

Gloria James had struggled to keep her family together after LeBron's birth and her mother's death. She had managed to keep food on the table and a roof over their heads, even though, for years, that roof belonged to others. She had finally gotten a home for the two of them in subsidized housing, all that they could afford. She had made certain he was able to practice basketball, to be with people who could help him, to have the opportunity to achieve a dream that, because of his unusual gifts, was attainable. And in his last season, when he would either turn professional or take a full-ride scholarship to the college of his choice, she wanted to make certain nothing went wrong.

Gloria had always traveled to wherever LeBron was playing, arranging interviews, helping friends get hotel rooms when they came to see him play, and generally managing the logistics of travel, the media, friends.

There was one instance, for example, when Gloria was in Washington, D.C. for the Capital Classic, the game in which LeBron received his third post-season MVP Award. It was a few hours before the game at the MCI Center, which was attended by NBA players Michael Jordan, Jerry Stackhouse, filmmaker Spike Lee, and rappers Jay-Z and Lil Bow-Wow.

Gloria was sitting at the Four Seasons Hotel bar sipping absentmindedly on a drink a friend had bought her to calm her. She was talking on one cell phone when another one rang. Someone who was coming from Akron wasn't able to get into their room at the hotel. There was some mix-up, and since Gloria had handled the reservations, she insisted upon correcting any problems even though the hotel staff would have happily helped.

Gloria ended her telephone conversation, then turned and said, "I'll be back. I have to go to the front desk and try to get this mess straightened out."

Before Gloria could even gather her purse, the cell phone rang again. This time, it was someone asking about tickets for the game. Gloria asked this person how many tickets they needed, let them know she would help them out, then gave the caller instructions on where to pick up the tickets.

Gloria looked stressed out, but she felt it was her obligation to take care of everyone. Even after the game, around 2 a.m., Gloria went to one of her friend's rooms and knocked on the door.

"Glo, what are you doing up so late," the friend said.

"I need to borrow a jacket so I can go down the street. The kids want something to eat." At 2 a.m. Gloria was still trying to take care of everyone.

So when LeBron got in the accident with his Hummer before the Walsh game and Senior Night, Gloria took over to try to get the situation taken care of so that LeBron could concentrate on the game. Only friends of the family knew what was going on, and the public blasted Gloria for not being with her son on Senior Night, one of the most important nights of his high school career.

Gloria's absence was noticed by the reporters.

"Where the hell is Gloria?" one asked to no one in particular.

"How could she do this to this kid?" asked someone else.

They assumed she was out partying or not paying attention to the time.

LeBron knew what was happening, he knew his mother might not arrive, but he began looking for her anyway. There was always a chance . . . always a chance.

There were whispers—maybe LeBron wasn't really so cool, so in control. He needed his mother there, wanted her that night, and he kept turning his head to see if maybe . . .

Officials at the school tried to stall the ceremony, hoping that Gloria would arrive at the last minute, but because the game was being televised live in pay-per-view, and because of time constraints, the ceremony had to begin. The public address announcer slowed down the announcements of the senior cheerleaders but it didn't help. It was time to start with the senior players.

Sian came out with his parents, Lee and Debra Cotton. Little Dru came out with his parents, Coach Dru and Carolyn Joyce. Willie and Romeo were announced with their escorts. And standing there alone in the corner, waiting to be introduced, was LeBron.

Eddie was in jail. Gloria was trying to fix the problem caused by LeBron's careless driving. LeBron stood alone in the gym, a child in the spotlight at once elated about the game, disappointed about his mother, and sure everyone in the bleachers believed he had been "abandoned."

Finally, in a moment that spoke more for the team, more for the years together, more for what the boys had accomplished than anything yet observed, LeBron's name was called. He was to walk across the floor to be acknowledged with his family, but his family was not there.

At that moment, the other members of the Fab Five— LeBron's teammates, brothers by choice—had the same thought. Each left his parents and walked to LeBron, startled to see the others doing the same.

The boys reached LeBron and encircled him with their arms. They stood that way for a moment, embracing for what they knew would be the last time in this high school gym.

At that moment they knew their lives had changed in ways that were unimaginable. This wasn't about a car or the NBA or what kind of shoes someone was going to wear or becoming an instant millionaire. This was about a transition in life they could never have anticipated and a future none could imagine.

They knew they would achieve almost everything they dreamed of doing in their high school years. They had climbed within sight of the mountaintop, and they had no idea if the peak of this mountain was the high point of their lives or a landmark on the way to still higher goals. They had come together as strangers. In the years since, they had created family, and happiness together through shooting hoops. Their stories, interwoven, altered each of their lives in ways that none of them, alone, could ever have achieved. They had given each other strength, and now it was all about to change.

But not before the walk that all seniors take with their families. Not before they showed their school, their fans, their parents, and each other that on that court they had become a family.

"LeBron James!" said the announcer.

And LeBron began his walk, his friends at his side, the crowd joyously burst into cheers.

After that game, LeBron looked back on four years.

"Today was a special day for me and my teammates, especially the seniors," he said, later. "We grew up together, did a lot of things together that nobody knew about. Before the press and the media came around, it was just me and my guys, us five. That's what I'm going to miss the most."

TWENTY-ONE

SHOE WAR

After the high school basketball season ended and with it LeBron's amateur career, the passing days were now just a count-down to riches for the 18-year-old. The courtship had been going on for months—years, actually; the only question remaining was, who will the bride be and how much is the dowry?

This wasn't about the NBA draft. It was time to talk shoes.

Professional sports is about selling merchandise. Fans may enjoy watching their favorite team win the big game, and players may enjoy seeing their names and faces plastered everywhere for a few years, but take away the revenues from the sale of shoes, jerseys, jackets, hats, beer, soft drinks, and candy bars, and the players would no longer be buying Hummers to ferry them from luxury hotel to mansion to exclusive nightclub. They'd be carpooling in Chevies, staying in budget hotels, and eating at McDonalds like the rest of us.

For a young man on the rise like LeBron, being a top prospect in this system means being given a free ticket to a world you once only fantasized about.

Sports apparel merchandising had been around for years when Chicago Bulls star Michael Jordan entered the NBA. But Jordan and his sponsor Nike would revolutionize the business.

By the time Jordan was at his prime, it was doubtful there was one boy in America who didn't know his number—23—or covet a jersey like Michael wore. LeBron James certainly did.

There was so much money to be made, with shoes that retailed for as much as $200 costing as little as $5 a pair to manufacture with cheap overseas labor. Even after shipping, distribution to the stores, and advertising, the profits were massive. Jordan made millions from the licensing agreement; Nike made far more.

Wanting to repeat and build on this successful marketing approach, and probably realizing that even the popularity of Michael Jordan wouldn't last forever, Nike—and its competitors—began signing ever more athletes to ever more lucrative endorsement contracts. To compete with one another, they started looking for talent at the source: kids.

LeBron was just the kind of kid they wanted. They had their eye on him—almost from the beginning.

Sonny Vaccaro helped change the world of sporting goods sales back in 1965, before Gloria James was even born.

Vaccaro, from Trattford, Pennsylvania, near Pittsburgh, developed the Dapper Dan Roundball Classic, a high school All Star game. He loved kids, loved basketball, and understood how much talent it took to star in the game. He had the ability to spot young talent improving so rapidly that, though they might still be in high school or not yet a college star, they were obviously bound for national recognition.

In 1978 Vaccaro began working for the athletic shoe companies. That business then was quite different from today. The money an athlete might earn, though relatively modest compared to today—often no more than $100,000 for the life of the endorsement—was still a large amount compared with what the average American was earning. It was also a sizeable portion of a professional athlete's earnings, since the routine seven-figure payments did not yet exist.

But the athletic shoe industry was on the verge of doing major business.

In 1984, Vaccaro was hired by Nike founder Phil Knight. It was the same year Vaccaro had a player named Michael Jordan endorse a new Air athletic shoe. However, the shoe was still generic. If you saw the first of what the kids would call "the Jordans," you wouldn't be able to tell the difference between that shoe and any other of similar design.

Vaccaro convinced Nike to make a unique shoe for Michael featuring a readily identifiable Jordan logo. The shoe business, and professional basketball endorsements, has never been the same since. He allegedly made a fortune for Nike, but in 1991 he moved to rival Adidas.

Vaccaro did well for Adidas, too. While LeBron was still a little kid barely learning the game, Vaccaro signed stars like Shaquille O'Neal, Kevin Garnett, and Vince Carter. He would sign Kobe Bryant and Tracy McGrady to endorsement deals before they were drafted, giving the company an inside track on future greats.

One method Vaccaro used was getting Adidas involved with schools, including high schools, whose the basketball team seemed unusually promising. They might be schools that were powerhouse sports schools year after year, or they might be schools showing a phenomenal, if temporary, blip of excitement.

The various men and women who represent their athletic equipment companies to schools are likely to talk about their love of the game, their desire to help kids both learn and compete, and the needs schools have with rising expenses and reduced funding. The talk is often true. Certainly Sonny Vaccaro had a well-established history of helping kids long before he went to work for Adidas.

However, when a sportswriter covers a season, he or she begins to notice little things, including the fact that the shoes being worn by the kids on the team—all donated—are clearly being used to make fashion and design statements.

When LeBron started his high school career, he was exactly the kind of kid the shoe companies targeted as a customer. In less than two years, though, he would become their top prize—to be battled over in one hotly contested "shoe war."

By LeBron's senior year, St. Vincent-St. Mary was playing 27 games in all—20 regular season games and seven postseason tournament games. The players were the talk of the state, regularly shown on television and photographed for the newspapers.

For Adidas, the company that had sponsored the team and provided much of its gear, the Irish became walking advertisements.

All the players were given one type of Adidas shoe at the start of the season. Then, several games into the season, the players came on the court wearing a different design of Adidas shoes. A few games later, a third design was on their feet. By the end of the 27-game run, the players had modeled several different styles of Adidas shoes for the fans. It was a fashion show based on success; Adidas was obviously hoping that as the youths continued to win, the kids in the crowd would notice that they were winning with Adidas.

The fact that the styles kept changing should have alerted observant fans that there was no magic pair of shoes. But they saw the brand on shoes—and headbands, uniforms, and bags—and Adidas was betting on success by association.

LeBron, like the other kids, accepted the free gear as was his right to do. But he insisted on being comfortable. If the new pair of shoes he was given didn't feel as comfortable as the previous samples, he would wear the older ones. Even so, none of the shoes ever became worn out. They saw too little use for that.

Sonny Vaccaro's edge over some of his competitors was his experience with amateur basketball camps and tournaments, several of which he had been involved with long before he was trying to sell clothing or any other product. True, he was trying to make money for Nike and then Adidas. But his first love was the game and the boys who were mastering it.

"I can tell you, and I mean it sincerely, I can tell you every kid who played for me," Vaccaro said. "I may miss them by a year or two but I could tell you the ones who died, the ones who went to jail, the ones who were druggies. The ones who went on to fame. The ones who are teaching. The ones who are stockbrokers. This is my life. When I speak to the kids and their parents and tell them that these kids have given me a wonderful life."

LeBron had caught Vaccaro's attention when he attended the ABCD Basketball Camp, sponsored by Adidas, during the summers before his junior and senior years. Vaccaro, who had worked with enough athletes of all calibers to know, knew that LeBron was going to go directly into the pros. While the affection he developed for the youth and the relationship that grew with Gloria and Eddie were genuine, it was clear that, when it came time for LeBron to consider signing a deal with an athletic wear company, Vaccaro would be Adidas's man at the negotiating table. He had positioned himself well on the inside track.

The jockeying to get in the good graces of LeBron and Gloria and Eddie began officially after the high school basketball season ended. The competition would be among the big three in athletic shoes: Nike, Adidas, and Reebok. Adidas, as expected, was first out of the gate. The company's pitch was partly personal—through Vaccaro's own overtures—and, in an odd twist, partly public.

In May of LeBron's senior year, cryptic messages appeared throughout Akron—on billboards, on busses, and elsewhere—with messages meant to influence LeBron's choice.

"Will you do something bigger than basketball?" read one sign. It made no mention of LeBron's name, but there was a small Adidas logo at the bottom corner in case LeBron and his family did not get the message.

"Do You Want to be the Next Superstar?" read another sign.

"Will You Use Fame to Change the World?"

"Will You Improve the Life of One Person, One Family, of an Entire Community?"

It was a strange ploy with which to influence a teenager, though not entirely inappropriate. While the appeal may have been too abstract for many inner-city high school ballplayers, LeBron was a parochial school kid who had religion as an integral part of his education. The Catholic high schools regularly encourage community involvement and working for the betterment of others. They want their students to have compassion, to volunteer and help the less fortunate. Still, the connection between altruism and selling shoes wasn't made very clear.

If Adidas thought they were taking the high road to LeBron, their expectations paled in comparison to those of consumer advocate Ralph Nader, who stepped up to fire his own salvo in the sneaker war.

Nader and a Washington-based organization called the League of Fans were concerned with the way athletic shoes are manufactured and the role of the companies in the lives of the workers. They appealed to LeBron to take up their fight. They wanted him to think about sweatshops, child labor, and everyone working long hours for a salary that would not be enough to pay for food in the United States. In a three-page letter to LeBron, they challenged him to make ethical demands a part of his upcoming endorsement deal.

The letter was faxed to LeBron in care of St. Vincent-St. Mary and signed by Nader and League of Fans director Shawn McCarthy. Part of the letter read:

"Nike and Adidas (along with Reebok) are synonymous with sweatshops in Third-World countries. Their products, typically manufactured by subcontracted companies, have become symbols of labor rights violations, paltry wages, forced overtime, and abuse for hundreds of thousands of workers. And despite pressure from around the world, Nike and Adidas still choose to maximize profits by undermining human rights standards. It does not matter which of these companies you ultimately choose to endorse, but we ask that you stand up for the people who will be manufacturing the products that will make you a wealthy man. If you demand in your contract, whether it is with Nike or Adidas, that they improve the conditions of the contracted factories that manufacture their products and that you have power to influence and review the working conditions for those who make the products you endorse, it will pressure the entire sports shoe and apparel industry to change."

Coach Dru Joyce was interviewed by *The Plain Dealer* to get his reaction to the letter. He was quoted as saying, "It is a noble request, but it is not one you make of an 18-year-old."

LeBron was not the first person to get such a letter. The Nader organization had previously attempted to get Michael Jordan and golf pro Tiger Woods to take a stand. Neither did.

Bud Shaw, a *Plain Dealer* sports writer, noted in his April 10, 2003 column, "There will be time for him to decide whether he wants to use his position to impact social change. Jordan decided long ago that he didn't want to be anything more than a fantastic player and money maker. When confronted once with instances of kids killing each other for their Air Jordans, he deflected criticism from Nike and blamed it on retailers hiking the price."

Shaw suggested there might be a different standard for a high schooler: "How about letting him [LeBron] be himself first, a teenager."

At the time, Nike had 38.9 percent of the athletic shoe business, according to industry trade journal *Sporting Goods Intelligence*. Adidas had roughly a fourth of that amount, at 9.7 percent. Reebok and New Balance did slightly better with market shares of 11.9 percent and 11.6 percent respectively.

Adidas was unlikely to fight for LeBron with money. Instead, they assured him that he would become a "global icon," according to Travis Gonzolez, public relations manager of Adidas America, Inc. They also showed LeBron drawings of the shoe they were designing for him, to prove how special he was.

Reebok had signed Alan Iverson, ultimately a good investment. Iverson was a rough kid who did *not* escape the trouble LeBron avoided. He was jailed while in high school and got in trouble with the law after joining the NBA. But he seemed to be straightening around, and his basketball work was brilliant. His screw-ups assured press coverage, and his improved character meant that Reebok could enhance their promotions without being burned.

But Reebok did not have vast sums of disposable income. They had previously withdrawn from talks with Los Angeles

Lakers star Kobe Bryant in order to spend less money up front for celebrity endorsements.

Nike, in addition to having the deepest pockets, had Michael Jordan, one of LeBron's favorite players, who frequently met with LeBron.

All the shoe companies wanted to sign LeBron before it came time for the NBA draft. It was clear that he would be the number one draft choice, and each company wanted to be connected with the winner.

Soon, real offers began to arrive.

Reebok was suddenly rumored to be back in the race. They now needed more NBA players on the roster and wanted to go high-profile—and were ready to spend the money necessary to do so. They reportedly offered LeBron an estimated $75 million (though the James family wouldn't confirm the amount).

Reebok officials were trying to convince LeBron that he would get the most personal attention from them. Nike, they said, had everyone and would be less attentive to him.

The bidding war for the teenager quickly became intense.

LeBron was flown in private jets to the corporate headquarters of the major shoe companies.

Reebok, at its U.S. division headquarters in Massachusetts, did not show shoe samples or personal designs. Instead, they talked concept, exploring ideas, trying to figure out what this 18-year-old would find exciting.

Adidas kept the four friends together, letting LeBron take several of his friends to their meeting two weeks later. The meeting was on the night of their senior prom, but LeBron felt the trip was more important, and his friends wanted to be there with him. (Later, when he knew he would not sign with them, LeBron repaid Adidas for the cost incurred by taking his friends on the trip.)

Nike had the last say. LeBron arrived in their headquarters

in Beaverton, Oregon, to find that Nike had already created two possible shoe lines with nine different models. However, he left uncertain about the financial numbers.

Finally, on May 21, a meeting was held in Akron's Radisson Hotel to settle a contract. Reebok CEO Paul Fireman flew out to be there. Representatives from Nike were on hand. LeBron's financial representatives were handling the negotiations.

In a curious twist, while the final counteroffers were being made on the shoe deal, LeBron signed a separate, relatively "minor" deal with Upper Deck, the trading card company, that instantly made the high schooler a millionaire and set for life. For a five-year exclusive deal on LeBron's likeness for their cards, the company paid him $6 million.

Suddenly, the shoe deal was no longer about money—for LeBron, anyway. He quickly made up his mind.

LeBron liked Nike. He liked their style. He liked Michael Jordan. He liked that they made shoes to show him. And he just wanted to be with Nike.

Reebok's Sonny Vaccaro had lost out again to the very endorsement legend he had once helped to create. He probably couldn't help sounding bitter in defeat.

"Nike has everybody—they have Kobe, Tiger, Michael Jordan, Vince Carter, now LeBron, and they can't use everybody," Vaccaro said. "What are they going to do? C'mon, there's only so many ads you can run on the TV screen . . . so many superstars you can use, so many shoes you can make. I told LeBron and Gloria if they just stuck close to me, they were going to get all the money they would ever want."

But after a point, what's another million dollars or two?

Nike offered less money than Reebok, but they had just won the war. That night, LeBron James, not yet graduated from high school, and not yet signed with a pro team, signed a deal with Nike for a reported $90 millon.

"I have two families now," LeBron said. "I have my real family—my mom, my dad, my friends, and my teammates, and I have my Nike family."

And both families had made him rich.

TWENTY-TWO

CHOSEN

The Cleveland Cavaliers in 2002–2003 were indisputably awful.

St. Vincent-St. Mary High School had two games shown on national television that season. The Cavaliers, none.

As the NBA season approached its end—mercifully, for Cleveland fans—the Cavaliers were top contender for the worst team in the NBA. There was one bright hope at the end of the long, dark season, however—the brass ring that just might be within grasp. Maybe, thought Cavs fans, just maybe we'll get LeBron.

The Cavaliers players were trying *not* to be the worst team in the NBA. They accomplished that mission—sort of. They *tied* for worst in the league, with a 17-65 record.

Cavs fans were not pleased.

In the waning weeks of the season, most had *wanted* their team to skid to the bottom of the list, because that would give them the best chance of getting the No. 1 pick in the NBA Draft Lottery. The Draft Lottery consisted of the 13 teams that did not make the playoffs. The team with the worst record had a 25 percent chance (250 out of 1,000) to get the No. 1 pick. The team with the second-worst record had the second-highest chance (225 out of 1,000), and so on.

When the Cavaliers won their last game of the season, they tied with the Denver Nuggets for the worst record. Instead of having the best chance at getting the first pick, they now had the same amount of chances (22.5 percent) as Denver. And with the way Cleveland's sports luck had so often gone in the past, everyone just knew the Cavaliers had blown it once again.

No one knew more about the Cavaliers' history of frustration than Austin Carr.

He, too, had the No. 1 draft pick of the worst team in the NBA 30 years earlier—the Cleveland Cavaliers.

He knew the road LeBron was taking, and now he was emotionally overwhelmed by the opportunity to be present for the journey.

Carr was an All-American guard at Notre Dame where he averaged 34.6 points a game in three seasons and scored 2,560 career points. He was the second college player in history, after Pete Maravich, to score more than 1,000 points in each of two seasons. He later averaged 21.2 points a game as a rookie with the Cavaliers, and more than 20 points a game in each of the next two seasons. However, a knee injury late in the 1974 season cut his playing time and reduced his productivity, and after nine seasons, Carr was selected by the Dallas Mavericks in the 1980 expansion draft and was later traded to the Washington Capitals, where he retired at the end of the season.

He was still one of Cleveland's more popular sports figures, and he was director of community business development for the Cavaliers when LeBron graduated from high school and prepared to be the first-round draft pick of the Cavaliers.

Carr had seen firsthand the worst the Cavaliers could experience, had helped them become respectable, and had witnessed the team's ups and downs since then.

Carr represented everything wonderful about the Cavaliers from their early days as a recent expansion team built around the young No. 1 pick and playing at the old Richfield Coliseum. Almost every Cavaliers fans from the early days would tell you that the Coliseum was special, especially during the 1975–1976 season, when coach Bill Fitch, the wide-collared, checkered-suited, bell-bottom wearing, fashion-disaster of a coach, won the NBA's Coach of the Year Award and led the young team to a first-place standing and its first exciting post-season in a phenomenon that became known as the "Miracle of Richfield."

In the early 1980s, Carr had watched owner Ted Stepian hire and fire coaches like New York Yankees owner George Steinbrenner—though with less than Yankee-like results—and come close to moving the team out of town.

In 1986, under the ownership of George and Gordon Gund, the Cavaliers began building a team capable of serious competition. In eight of the next nine seasons the Cavaliers made the playoffs, and in the 1991–1992 season they earned a trip to the Eastern Conference Finals against Chicago.

The Bulls won that series, four games to two. Cavaliers fans remember the sixth and decisive game all too well. It was Michael Jordan sticking it to the Cavaliers with "The Shot," as it became known to Cleveland fans. As the buzzer started to sound, Jordan, players in his face, dropped fans' jaws with a jumper from the foul line, winning the game.

But recently the glory days of the Cavaliers had faded and the franchise seemed hopelessly mired in losing basketball.

Now Carr was watching, as hopeful as any fan, on May 22, 2003, as the much-anticipated Draft Lottery took place in the Secaucus, New Jersey, headquarters of NBA Entertainment.

Adding to the drama, the NBA Draft Lottery would be broadcast live as a half-hour special just before the playoff game between Detroit and New Jersey. It was the first live broadcast since the lottery was introduced in 1985.

LeBron, his teammates, family, and friends gathered at the Radisson Hotel in downtown Akron to watch the lottery. It was a private gathering, family and friends only inside the 19th-floor ballroom.

Members of the local and national media were waiting downstairs inside the hotel bar. The televisions inside the bar were tuned to the draft special, and the anticipation was mounting, especially for members of the local media, because they knew how important it was for the Cavaliers to get the No. 1 pick.

Tony Rizzo, a sports anchor for WJW TV, the Fox Broadcasting affiliate in Cleveland, was pacing back and forth by the bar. He was that rare television personality who had lived and worked in the same city for almost his entire his career. He was also a fan, a man who wanted the Cavaliers to have the chance for a turnaround and knew LeBron was the best hope available. One 18-year-old high school kid on the cusp of manhood would not win the games, but the excitement generated by a team obviously making an effort to become a contender could change the city dramatically.

Some of the press felt the same excitement but were pretending to stay cool. Some truly did not care; they were in Cleveland today, Chicago tomorrow, maybe New York the following week.

NBA deputy commissioner Russ Granik started opening the envelopes that detailed the order for picking. As in a multi-million dollar beauty contest, he opened the envelope listing the 13th draft pick first. Then came the 12th, the 11th. Some of the press dutifully noted the order. Most did not. They were listening for one team's name. And every turn that it didn't come caused the anticipation to mount. Finally, there were only two teams whose names had not yet been drawn—Memphis and Cleveland. Unbelievable: the Cavaliers still had a chance.

"And the second pick in the NBA 2003 lottery goes to . . . the Memphis Grizzlies," Granik said.

The Radisson Hotel bar exploded in a frenzy of screaming, hugging, and dancing about the room. Rizzo was probably the most animated among the sports writers, but the mask of indifference worn by many of the other reporters disappeared.

The actual draft was about a month away, but everyone knew that LeBron was going to the No. 1 pick. Cleveland had won the lottery, and LeBron was a Cavalier in waiting.

While all this was taking place, the camera shifted to Austin Carr. He was caught hugging a friend, tears streaming down his face, remembering the past, seeing the present, and anticipating the future.

"A lot of people teased me about crying," Carr said, "but I was so happy that we got a young man like him, and I just got caught up in the emotions. I knew what he was going to mean to this franchise and this city. After a while, you just get tired of cities and teams beating you and we finally beat 28 other teams in something."

A few days later, LeBron visited Gund Arena for a Cleveland Rockers WNBA game, and he was wearing a throwback Cavaliers' jersey. It was Austin Carr's No. 34.

"I didn't see it but I heard about Austin Carr crying, so when I wore his jersey to the Rockers game, it was a tribute to him," LeBron said. "I think Austin Carr is a big reason why the Cavaliers' organization is still going . . . him and Mark Price, Brad Daugherty, and Larry Nance. People forget about the days when they were good."

Carr, hearing about what LeBron did, said, "That's why LeBron is so special. Most kids his age don't understand the history of what has brought the league to where it is now.

When I came in I knew Jerry West and I knew about all of those guys because I studied the game. That tells you where he is as an individual."

Carr knew a little about LeBron's future, too.

Though there had been less hype and less money 30 years earlier for his selection—a five-year deal, $1.5-million, plus a "stipend" from Nike—Carr was taunted by both teammates and opponents as the "bonus baby." He didn't dare have an off night. He had to play each game as though it was the most important of his career. He noted that LeBron was facing a season of 82 games and he would have to both fight hostility and prove himself with each one.

In June, Carr, along with members of the media, Cavaliers coach Paul Silas, and general manager Jim Paxson watched LeBron's first official workout at Gund Arena. Silas put LeBron through several different shooting drills, making him shoot from different spots on the court. He also had LeBron shoot free throws between drills. It was just LeBron, Silas, and two trainers on the court near the basket. The media members were all gathered at midcourt.

After the workout, which lasted about an hour, Paxson and Silas met with the media.

"We're still taking him No. 1, I can tell you that," Paxson joked. He also was asked if LeBron would step right in and give the Cavaliers what they desperately needed—a point guard.

Paxson was hesitant to anoint LeBron the point guard of the future. "We're focusing in on the wrong thing. LeBron is a basketball player, and it's up to the coaching staff to figure out how they want to utilize him. He still needs to get a feel of the NBA game."

LeBron's workout wasn't anything spectacular, but Austin Carr praised LeBron. "I don't see many shortcomings," he said. "His jump shot . . . all it will take is time. If he wants to put the time in the gym, everything will be fine. The biggest thing he'll have to work on is his defense, because he'll have to play against guys like Tracy McGrady, who can bring it every night."

LeBron understood that. "I'll play anywhere they want me to play, so if that means playing point guard, I'll play point guard. Now, the problem will be guarding those point guards," he said with a smile.

Austin Carr also said he liked the way LeBron handled the ball during the drills. "He has mobility, strength, quickness, and good short dribbles, which I didn't think he had from watching him play high school ball, because no one really challenged him. A guy his size who can have those quick short bursts, you can go where you want to go with the ball."

Paul Silas said he was impressed with LeBron's drive and competitiveness. "I liked everything about him, his demeanor, everything."

LeBron said about Silas, "I get the feeling that he's a great guy. I'm learning about him and he's learning about me so once our relationship grows, I think it's going to be a great bond. I'm looking forward to learning a lot more about the game from him and a lot more about life."

On June 26, 2003, the Cleveland Cavaliers made it official and announced LeBron James as their first pick for the new season. NBA Commissioner David Stern made the announcement from New York's Madison Square Garden. Even though the announcement was a formality, an obvious anticlimax, in Cleveland 10,107 fans watched the ESPN broadcast from seats in Gund Arena (more fans than had attended the Cavaliers final games of the season), cheering the announcement wildly. Streamers and confetti fell from the ceiling, and on the floor, a band burst into music.

The second-round draft choice, almost ignored by the fans, was Jason Kapono, a UCLA forward who averaged 16.8 points per game and made 44.6 percent of his three point attempts during his four years in college. Kapono appeared to be a fine selection for rebuilding the team. But all eyes were on LeBron.

LeBron James had worked his way to the top, then discovered it was a resting place before the next mountain. This time he would start the climb alone. No longer would he travel with the the teammates of his youth, who grew into young manhood alongside him, who nurtured one another and challenged LeBron's physical and mental skills in preparation for the leap to the NBA. No longer would he have the comfort of a protective school environment. No longer would his mother and Eddie be so physically close and so influential in his life. He would be traveling with strangers—some formerly his heroes and now his colleagues, all of whom would be looking for him to prove himself worthy of their company. He would be facing new business relationships inside a closed society of wealth and status. And he would be facing the wildly hopeful expectations of a city of fans (and the attendant news media) starved for success in the basketball arena.

Now, LeBron would move out into a world as distant from Hickory Street and Elizabeth Park and Spring Hill as he could imagine. He was never going to worry about money again. He would never be anonymous. He would never be able to go anywhere without being recognized. Such freedom, as frightening as it is empowering, comes to few people anywhere in the world. Not even LeBron could know where it would lead him or how he was going to fare. He was going to be booed. He was going to be cheered. And he was going to know what it was like to reach for the top at an age when other players are just starting to finely hone their skills in anticipation of another four years before their drafts.

Now, as he had in so many challenging situations before, LeBron seemed unfazed and optimistic and prepared for success. After all, he would always feel most at home on the basketball court.

"This is going to be great," he said. "My boys get to come watch me play, my family and all the Cavs fans. We're finally going to get more life in this city. I think what I'm going to do for this team is make us a family."

ACKNOWLEDGMENTS

There are so many people I have to thank for helping make this book possible.

First, to my wife of 12 years, Tricia: you were the one who always had faith in me and my writing when others weren't so sure I could take on such a challenging project. Thanks for being there and putting up with all the cigar smell and all the late-night hours of me listening to Steely Dan while I banged away at my computer.

Also, to Donald and Walter: your incredible words have inspired me for years.

To my children, Trey, Christian, Brooke, and Cameron,: thanks for being so understanding when "Daddy" had to miss your youth basketball and baseball games to get the book done. You guys have made me very proud.

To all of my family—the Morgans, Lyons, Leslies, and Lixiviates: when I had doubts and was feeling down, you all were there to pick me up and I love you all.

To my agent, Faith Hamlin from New York: you took a chance on a first-time author and I'll forever be grateful.

To my publisher, David Gray: you enlightened me and frightened me at the same time, but damn, you're good.

To Patty Burdon: a wonderful, wonderful lady who was a friend, a supporter, a motivator…an inspiration for me from Day One. Without your help, this book wouldn't have been possible.

To the *Beacon Journal* management and staff: thanks for your support, especially Jan Leach, James Crutchfield, Larry Pantages, Sheldon "Shelly" Ocker, and Terry Pluto. Also, thanks to David Giffels, "Mr. Devo," my Beacon Journal colleague who believed in me right from the start. When I questioned whether or not I could write a book about a subject like LeBron, David was the one who said, "David, you're a good writer. You can write this book by yourself." Thank you, my friend.

To Curt Gonya, my good friend from Youngstown State University who probably knows more about sports than anyone I know and was my sounding board at every turn: Curt, you're in the wrong business, dude.

To Ted Schwarz: you came through in the clutch, and as my writing coach you helped me grow in ways you can never imagine.

To Coach Tressel: even though I didn't play football for you while we were at YSU, you always took time to share words of wisdom with me about being successful in life on and off the playing field. That's why you are a champion. Hey Coach Tressel, "I blue-vased it!"

To Charles "Chuck" Adams, my "Little Brother": we've been through so much together during our days in Warren—from grade school to Harding (before they were the Raiders.) As two sports fanatics, we always talked about one of us writing a book that someone would want to read and we finally did it. This is as much your book as it is mine. You always had my back and you were always there for me. Whenever I needed anything, *anything* at all, you never failed to come through. You'll always be my sidekick, and the next time I see LeBron, I'll tell him you want to kick his butt in PlayStation.

To Al Gordon, my personal Bill Gates: thanks so much for your computer wisdom.

To my man, Phil Masturzo, or as the players at St. Vincent-St. Mary called him, "Feel Good": thanks for your incredible and professional photos which brought visual life to this story.

To all of those who have meant so much to me over the years, especially the North End Crew in Warren—Billy Rek, Brian Thomas, Mackey Johnson, Joe Discerni, Billy Isabella, and Ham: "This Book's For You!"

And finally, to baby Jacob Matthew Leslie, who was blessed with life for only a few hours before leaving us on June 23, 2002: we all love and miss you, especially your mom, Julie, your dad, Steve, and your older brother, Daniel. Not a day goes by that they don't think about you. Daniel says he'll score a touchdown for you when he's the running back at Ohio State.